HEALTHY
AND FIT FOREVER
A JOURNEY THAT WILL CHANGE YOUR LIFE

HEALTHY AND FIT FOREVER

A JOURNEY THAT WILL CHANGE YOUR LIFE

M. E. OGI

PH
PASSIONHABIT

CONTENTS

CONTENTS

ACKNOWLEDGMENTS

For all the inspiration and encouragement I received during the books creation process. I am extremely grateful and appreciative for all who have supported me throughout. I am grateful for recognizing and contributing to the cause of helping others. For that, I am blessed:

To my family in particular my wife who has supported not only the writing of the book but for all the successes we achieved throughout the 30 plus years together. I could not have reached my goals without her wisdom and insight. A special recognition to my son who inspired me to push through the many hurdles during the development of the book always reminding me that helping others is the focus and the motivation.

To my special and gifted editorial angel Susan S. She has been so instrumental not only in the editing of book but for doing the work without hesitation during her personal time. I thank her for our friendship and the desire to help me so I can help others. Without her contribution, the completion of the book would not have been possible.

To all the inspiring motivators that I discovered during the book creation journey. Although I have never met them personally, they became my inspiration to follow my passion to share knowledge and to help others reach success. I am grateful of their teaching and sharing of knowledge to the mass which I was fortunate to recognize and act upon. My appreciation goes out to Mr. Proctor, Mr. Ziglar, Mr. Robbins, Mr. Rohn, Mr. Eker, Mr. Tracy, Mr. Nightingale, Mr. Dyer, Mr. Wooden, Mr. Carmichael, and Mr. Burchard

ACKNOWLEDGMENTS

To all my friends that have encouraged me throughout the years and entrusted me to listen and apply the messages of improvement and achievement within their own mental and physical challenges and accomplishment. I appreciate the ear that John consistently offered without hesitation and his words of encouragement and compassion. A special thanks to Jose for reaching out and entrusting me without doubt to take the path and achieve a healthy and fit life style.

Finally, for all who will and have taken the book journey, a special acknowledgement for entrusting me to make this life style change to better yourself so you and your loved ones can share and enjoy your life for the years to come. I am extremely grateful for your contribution by purchasing the book to help those children in need giving them a glimmer of hope of a normal life.

THIS BOOK IS NOT FOR YOU

- If you bought this book to lose weight in two weeks or are searching for a trendy quick-fix diet and exercise routine then this book is NOT for you.
- If you bought this book for an upcoming class reunion or to fit into a fairy-tale wedding dress by this weekend then this book is NOT for you.
- If you bought this book purely as an instructional "how-to" book on exercise and diet then this book is NOT for you either.

The information in this book is for those reaching 40 and beyond who want the best insurance possible that they won't be slaves to pharmaceuticals, walkers, canes, nursing homes, or the insipid images of what life "used" to be like as they gracefully age. It's never too late to reap the benefits of improving your health regardless if you're 30, 60, or 80, but making lifestyle changes does get more difficult the longer you wait. Your future healthy self absolutely depends on your choices today.

Being healthy and fit is not about having six-pack abs or a head-turning beach body. In fact, I don't remember the last time I took my shirt off in public. It's about training your mind to condition your body so you can have the quality of life you deserve for the second half of your life. This book is purely about how to train your mind to start--and continue--a healthy and fit lifestyle for the rest of your life. Doing this doesn't require mind-altering hypnosis, meditation, or some form of motivational talk. But it does require you to work smarter, not harder. Yes, I will get into a cliff-note view on nutrition and exercise during the journey, but the initial focus will be to overcome the mental challenges of starting, obtaining and sustaining healthy living.

Most everyone has the physical ability to become fit and healthy, yet 80% of people today do not meet the recommended physical activity level. Why do 95% of people, regardless of age, break their New Year's Resolution after just two weeks? And why do 95% of them who join a gym never go back after a few visits? This book will help you avoid becoming a part of the 95%.

It's a given that everyone wants to be healthy and not overweight, which is why those fitness bands and watches are so popular. Although measuring your vitals or how far you walk are steps (get it, "steps") toward the right direction, they are just a small piece of the total wellness picture. The reason why you are in any given state is due to your routine and its frequency. It has nothing to do with your body failing you, but everything to do with how you think and how the mind receives instant pleasure with consistent frequency. Every day, you succumb to normalcy motivated by an immediate comfort that you have done for several years. This is a mental blockade, a habit if you will, that can—and often does—cause physical havoc eventually.

The essence of the book is about how to systematically overcome mental blockades by training your mind to trick your body to do what you want it to do with minimal effort and time. This can be accomplished without any equipment or hefty expenses, but it does require you to re-read some sections to refresh and reference yourself when you stray.

With this book in your hands, there are no more excuses because I removed all the blame such as not having enough time, being too old, too busy, feeling helpless or having physical limitations. As we start and travel through this journey together, you will find this book is not only about becoming healthy, but about specific principles and methods that can be applied to accomplish anything you strive for and desire.

This book is not about aesthetics, but a book for those who want to live and enjoy life for many years to come. It is targeting the men and women who have years of life experience that are reaching middle age and beyond who are at a point where being healthy and fit is a must. We will embark on a 21-day journey together, getting to know each other, and just enjoying the many interesting concepts and technics that we will discover along the way. I promise the trip will be simple, easy, and fun, but very effective and progressive. Don't get me wrong, there are a few parts that will challenge your comfort zone, but together we will overcome and reach our healthy and fit destination.

For those who want to advance and progress beyond the book's 21 days or have not reached their habit goals soon after, you will have exclusive access to a free membership portal at no cost. This is a continuation of the book and will only make sense for those of you that have finished it. I did this for the sake of passion to help you achieve health, fitness and maximize your quality of life for the years to come. Speaking of passion, I want to share the reason for writing the book, so you can have a clear understanding of my intent and purpose (must read).

WHY WRITE THIS BOOK?

I always thought I had a lazy constitution, trying to achieve maximum benefit using the least amount of effort and time. I felt less of a person because I was preached that you must work really hard to achieve anything worthwhile. As I reached middle age, I started to realize that I wasn't being lazy, but in fact was just looking for ways to achieve results with the least amount of suffering and pain that can sustain the passing of time. I also noticed that things that were difficult to achieve were too complicated and when broken down, and simplified, became easier to start, continue and finish. When I got overwhelmed because something seemed too difficult, fear put the brakes on me when attempting a life changing goal. One may say that these are signs of pure laziness and not having the drive to push yourself to commit. The truth is that being unhealthy and unfit has nothing to do with laziness or lack of commitment, but a lack of knowing the direct route of how and what to do.

When people think about what they need to do to lose weight, many envision eating rabbit food and being tortured for hours on a hamster wheel. Thoughts of suffering and pain paralyze them from even attempting to exercise. Even before they start, they are already setting themselves up for failure as they think about the total amount of sacrifice it will take. This bitter taste causes a negative perception that begins to instill deep in the subconscious mind that will only make the journey seem impossible. Even if you are pumped to hit the gym and strive to lose 20 pounds, after a few attempts, reality sets in and you realize that it is no fun. Excuses bubble to the forefront such as "I don't have the time" or "I have kids to take care of."

These are valid reasons, and I sincerely respect all the men and women who valiantly tried but just weren't able to continue. Women especially seem to have it harder than men because they are perfectly designed to create life, but at the same time, motherhood puts a tremendous toll on their bodies before, during and after giving birth. Now add in the aging process as you lead up to your late 30s into your 40s, 50s 60s and beyond trying everything and anything to become healthy and fit. The odds are so stacked against you that you begin to raise the white flag and say, "I'll try next year."

I, too, reached that point many times until one day I completely reversed my thoughts and asked myself: "How can I redirect my negative energy to achieve positive results?" More importantly, how can I continually apply this way of thinking so it will benefit me both mentally and physically for the long haul in life?

I watched and learned from those who achieved great success realizing that there were no hidden secrets. I discovered it came down to what I already know, but overlooked and did not apply. The common theme was that everything you want to master is always difficult at the beginning and as you practice or repeat the action over and over, it becomes easier as time goes on. Okay, not revolutionary, but why is that concept so difficult when it comes to health and fitness and why do the majority of people never reach their New Year's resolution goal.

Well I took on the challenge to find out why and figured out that it is much more cerebrally methodical (mind game) than just going to the gym and eating healthy. It wasn't the lack of will power or getting your butt off the couch, but more about the process and managing the intricate relationship between your mind and body. Wait, if you are thinking that this is a holistic book about meditation or hypnosis then I am leading you down the wrong mental path. This is a book about being an average human being with all the idiosyncrasies, shortcomings and challenges we all have and completely changing the way you think, approach and overcome the hurdles of who, what, why and how.

Before we begin, there needs to be a level of trust between you and I that when we embark on this journey, you need to believe that my only intention is to help you become a better you. It's all about what can we do today that will manifest into an awesome quality of life for the years to come. My purpose in life is to share and help people achieve the same mental success of becoming fit and healthy that will last for the rest of your life. Nothing more and nothing less and nothing temporary, but purely permanent. Overall, the book is about helping you learn not only how to fish, but how to think like a fish so you can catch plenty of fish consistently and forever. Oh, and how to cook the fish as well (more to come).

On that note, let's get started. The beginning section of the book is extremely critical, and before I dive into the meat and sweet potatoes (smile) of how to reach your health and fitness objective, the make or break of success will stem from what and how you think, how and why you feel, and how to condition the mind to achieve. Becoming healthy may appear to be purely a physical demand, but it is unequivocally 90% mental and 10% action. Every successful person be it a billionaire, athlete, celebrity, CEO, or overall impactful individual who has proven results, will tell you that before you work on how to get there, you must work on yourself specifically your mental state, outlook and overall mindset.

When I went on my journey several years back of how to become successful, I researched those who achieved it and wanted to know their secret and magic formula. After a decade of research and tapping into all the interviews of those who are high achievers and successful in health, wealth and relationships, I discovered that there were no secrets, no higher intelligence, no hidden book of knowledge. The one common theme that resonated from all of those interviewed was they all had a certain thought pattern and mindset they followed to achieve success.

The mindset is the same mental conditioning that sports' teams have such as envisioning winning the championship game before it even starts. They go as far as to emotionally celebrate the victory, feeling all the joy and excitement of winning including holding up the trophy above their heads prior to the game. You too are going to be mentally prepared prior to starting the 21-day journey by feeling the emotions and excitement of achieving your health and fitness success.

The following chapter is extremely critical because without understanding and applying the mental prep work, you will not be able to achieve the book's intent. Also, changing your mindset will not only get you to a healthy and fit state, but will give you success in everything else you always desired to achieve. So if you pay attention and apply, you will become unstoppable.

Just a side note: When you finish the book, please pass it along to others in need. It will not only benefit the person you care about, but it will help parents and grandparents guide their kids and grandkids to be healthy and fit early on. This will also allow me to continue on with my crusade to expand my outreach to more people in need. Lastly, a significant portion of the proceeds from every book sale will be donated to an organization that focuses on helping children in need, both financially and medically, so they can have a chance to live a normal, happy life.

HOW TO USE THE BOOK

The book is broken down into two parts both critical stepping stones to manage your behavior to achieve a lifelong healthy and fit lifestyle.

As mentioned, Part I covers how to alter your mindset to successfully prepare your brain to combat the many reasons why most fail to start, continue, and sustain a long-lasting healthy life. The road to any life-changing goal stems from overcoming the mental challenges of resistance and barriers. Your mental outlook either negative or positive always dictate your attitude, motivation, and reactions. All achievements manifest from within one's self. Success and failure are dependent upon your ability to overcome your inner voice that often self-sabotages your accomplishments. For those of you who fall under the over-achiever spectrum, you may be able to go straight to Part II. For the rest of us, who struggle along and find it difficult to achieve and sustain continuance, consistency, and lastingness, I recommend reading Part I on how to prepare, manage, and overcome. It is going to be an eye-opening experience when you understand and master the essence of mental practice. Once understood and applied, you will become in control and unstoppable for the rest of your life.

The fact remains that getting healthy and fit forever is a life-altering event requiring a complete shift in awareness, attitude, and behavior. This is something you cannot do overnight as it takes time and patience as well as a comprehensive plan that is direct and effective. It requires a paradigm shift of your thought process leveraging knowledge, experience and methodical adjustments toward change. In the words of Stephen R. Covey, "We can only achieve quantum improvements in our lives as we quit hacking at the leaves of attitude and behavior and get to work on the root, the paradigms from which our attitudes and behaviors flow."

Part II is the actionable portion of the book where you embark on a 21-day journey and apply what you mentally prepared for into action. The golden key to achievement is not brute forcing your way to success but to methodically chip away bit by bit each day until it becomes a way of life. Watching others achieve success may appear to have happened overnight, but behind the scenes, they spent years even decades of practice and training consistently that lead them to this point. No pill, fad, or fancy diet or equipment will get you there, only a strategic plan of action that fits your individual strengths and weaknesses.

Along the journey, each day you will be adding valuable bits of knowledge to your mental database while adapting to new concepts and ways to improve and maximize your effectiveness. You will also discover along the journey how to leverage your strengths and understand your weaknesses to overcome personal adversity, hurdles, and barriers. Each chapter is designed to be read and performed daily at a specific time. You will get an overwhelming urge to read ahead because it is so riveting (wink), but it is imperative you find the strength to refrain regardless of how eager you are to move forward. Each consecutive day is a building block of the previous day requiring you to absorb the content and normalize the actions. Although discussed throughout, the 21-day journey is not merely about how or what to eat, how much calories you burn, or what exercise to conduct. The true essence behind the book is about how to train the mind to instruct your body to sustain. Your current way of life was built by consistent daily actions that took years to formulate a behavior that caused the results of your current state. We are going to use the same process but arm you with the knowledge to be in control of your decisions while simultaneously reverse engineer the old and perpetuate you forward toward a new direction.

Both parts are reliant upon each other as the mind dictates the action while the body systematically follows along respectively. Once you complete the book, many who followed along step by step will have the foundation and knowledge to start living a healthy and fit life soon after. But for most of us, on the other hand, will still need some additional support beyond the book to reach your goal of permanently ingraining this new lifestyle. As I alluded earlier, I created a supplemental website that continues where we left off embarking you for an additional 21 days that will expand upon what you learned throughout the book. The site is exclusive, private, and the membership is complimentary for those who have completed the book. It was designed to continue on the day after the book, starting with day 22 while using the familiar nightly and progressive format for both the movements and nutritional lessons.

All in all, life is a journey of many challenges, and as we age, it becomes even more so especially when we face health and medical issues. My hope, dream, and passion are to help those struggling, discouraged, and frustrated to find a simple path to begin a journey toward a healthy, fit, and enjoyable life forever.

PART I
It's a Mind Game

LOOKS DON'T MATTER

There is a specific reason why I decided to target a particular age group rather than a one-size-fits-all approach. It's because as we age, our inside (health) becomes more valuable to us than our outside (aesthetics). When you're in your teens, 20s and early 30s, workouts are designed to impress from the outside. Now that you're reaching or passing your 40s, 50s and 60s, your workouts need to focus on improving your health so your quality of life remains in good shape (yeah). If you do not take action to begin focusing on becoming healthy and fit now, then there will be inevitable medical consequences down the road (boo). At around 40, your body will begin to give hints that you are aging such as a few gray hairs, having difficulty reading fine print and stiffness when you get out of bed. Not really life threating, but it is a wakeup call that your body is aging and there is a physiological decline as the year's progress.

What is concerning are the less obvious signs that can, and will be, life threatening if you do not wake up and become proactive. These ticking time bombs are hidden and will affect the quality of life as you go through the rest of the aging process. There will be a decline of energy that leads to less movement. In turn, you may experience unforeseen medical issues at a time where making a lifestyle and behavior change is even more challenging and seems next to impossible. Let me scare you straight by listing the following and well-documented changes that are happening right now.

- Metabolism (the way you process food) slows down – Increase visceral fat (Muffin Top, Beer Belly)
- Muscle sarcopenia (muscle loss) – Frailty, weakness, less stamina
- Loss of growth hormones (testosterone, insulin) – Hair loss, declining libido, lethargic
- Protein-synthesis impairments (inability to turn protein into energy, causing declining muscle growth)
- Loss of bone density (osteoporosis and osteoarthritis) – Fractures and arthritis
- Balance issues (less stability, lateral movement difficulties) – "I've fallen, and I can't get up."

At this age, you have a career, kids are growing, you have financial stability and you are busy with day-to-day responsibilities. Up until this point, you have been taking care of everyone else, but because of that worthy act, you forgot to take care of yourself. When you were younger, the body was able to handle the physical demand of unhealthy abuse and stress, but now as an older self, things take longer to recover as the body is less forgiving. From this point forward, your metabolism and energy begins to slow down to a crawl. And if you don't make a change, you will accelerate the inevitable results of getting overweight and unhealthy.

My major concern for you is not what you look like today, but how your life will be as you age into retirement and for the rest of your Medicare life. The kicker is that you may think it is a long time from now or you will get around to it, or simply think it is too late, but those thoughts are wrong because a year from now you will kick yourself for not starting today. Let me put it bluntly: Everything you do today will have a compounding effect on your future self, both bad and good. If you are told that you are unhealthy and you ignore it, then expect the years to come with many challenges and dependencies on drugs, doctors, hospitals, walkers, canes and your independence. It is not apparent now if you are starting this journey at 40, but those of you that are older know how the body has changed and know exactly what I am talking about.

Health and fitness are purely a mental game between you and yourself, and it requires years to formulate what works for you. Think of it as building a relationship with someone, trying to get to know one another, discovering each other's idiosyncrasies and shortcomings (dating). It is challenging and will take time to get the groove going and reach a level of emotional harmony (marriage). Becoming healthy and fit and the purpose of this journey will be similar, but you will be building a relationship between your mind and body. This, too, will require an understanding of your individualism, characteristics, peculiarities, beliefs and an overall understanding of how your mind and body work together through the laws of cause and effect.

Altering your behavior and becoming educated about how your body works, how it reacts to food, as well as how to train your mind to burn fat while building muscle is the results behind the journey. You already know what causes one to be unhealthy and unfit, and you know what the literature says you need to do. Things like stop overeating, drink more water, exercise with weights, don't eat sugar, get plenty of sleep, don't stress out, don't smoke and drink, no junk food are all well documented, but nothing explains how to do this.

If you truly want to live a life of quality with minimal health issues and sustain mobility for the rest of your life, you will need to approach this with wisdom through working smarter and not harder. First you need to change your perspective. Much like an athlete needs to prepare mentally for a game, you need to prepare mentally for this journey. Athletes always stay focused and when distracted or discouraged they talk themselves back repeatedly until they return back to thinking of what's happening now. More important, enjoy the journey of new discoveries of interesting facts, about who you really are and who you want to become. Rather than concentrating on what the scale says, focus on learning and moving forward one step at a time. This is a mind game and a competition against yourself, so let's get mentally prepared so we can enjoy the journey together.

THE JOURNEY TO BECOME FIT

Every successful person starts with an achievement vision. There are two parts of the brain that dictates a person's eating behavior each and every day. One of them is called the conscious mind and the other is the subconscious mind. The conscious mind is used when making everyday decisions such as what to eat, where to go and when to get there. Your subconscious mind dictates your emotional reactions based on how you have programmed your mind through past experiences. Your subconscious mind has been trained to knee jerk a response based on a pattern of how you picture and view your inner self. Your subconscious mind cannot detect what is real or fake. It operates on your perceived truth not facts. So the picture of who you are, or in this case what you have physically become, is instilled deep in your mind and you behave accordingly. You have created an unconscious mission statement based on your subconscious mind that you programmed throughout your life. The picture has unconsciously dictated your acts and emotions and led you to continue doing what fits that image of yourself that strangely gives you this feeling of familiarity. Even though you know that being unhealthy is not a good thing, it has become a familiar place that strangely gives you comfort. It is like struggling to find a place you've never been before versus the calming emotion of revisiting somewhere you've already been.

When you close your eyes, do you see yourself as an unhealthy or an overweight person? If so, then that is your subconscious pursuit. That will need to change before we continue as it will be next to impossible to achieve the book's purpose and objective. Your conscious mind is acting upon that image so the decisions you make always move you toward that image regardless of how hard you try to fight it. You continue to do the same unhealthy behaviors because it fits that image of how you envision yourself and thus offers comfort because it is safe and familiar. The path to success on this journey is to change your mental picture of yourself from an overweight, frustrated, and helpless person to an image of a fit and healthy reflection of yourself.

With this new image, your conscious mind will act, decide and move toward that belief thus changing your subconscious attitude. It is similar to a self-fulfilling prophecy that causes a prediction to come true because you expect it to come true. If you don't change the attitude and mental picture of yourself, this journey to success will be like paddling upstream going nowhere. As silly and unbelievable as this may seem, making this mental adjustment will guarantee to change your behavior and add momentum to progress rapidly forward like paddling downstream. Some call it the call to the universe coupled with the law of vibration, meaning what you don't want or what you want dictates your behavior, attitude, skepticism, positivity, and motivation to attract, pursue, and achieve. Similar to being confident in order to perform better in sports, dating and in life.

So let's start by envisioning your ideal image of how you would like your body to look. Fantasize that you have already achieved it and begin to feel the emotions of excitement and self-pride of having that fit and healthy body. You must do this mind-altering exercise over and over until you truly instill that mental picture in your head and really feel the emotional excitement of having that desired outcome. Then really believe you have achieved it and feel the positive emotions and excitement of finally building that body. Imagine yourself walking along the shores of Hawaii feeling proud of all the actions you took to be free from embarrassment and insecurities you may have felt before. Imagine yourself looking fantastic with every fitted shirt or skirt you try on instead of the usual frumpy choices you normally buy to hide behind your clothes.

The weird and strange secret behind this process is to trick your subconscious mind into thinking that you are already healthy and fit. The deep part of the mind will accept this and slowly remove the automatic response of your daily familiarity and comfort and shift toward the pursuit of action and achievement. You are changing your mental attitude at a higher level by removing the deep rooted self-pity and excuse-ridden attitude to an action-oriented, enthusiastic and assertive approach. The old mind is used to thinking of all the reasons why you became overweight and unhealthy (reactive) and the new you will begin thinking of what actions you need to take to achieve a healthy and fit body (proactive).

Eventually, the mind will discard the noise that prevents you from moving forward and embrace an attitude of always doing something rather than nothing. Once you get to this point, you have the mental mindset to move on to the next step and begin the journey. Successful people focus less on achieving and more on becoming.

8

HEALTH IS A PRIORITY, NOT A PRIVILEGE

If you list all the things you find important in life you would probably put down family, friends, career, finances and health. Most likely, health slowly settled toward the bottom of your list. But if you think about it, when you are unhealthy and sick, nothing else really matters. You feel so miserable that all you want to do is stay in bed, get heavily medicated and just sleep. When your health suffers, it prevents you from enjoying all that matters. Period. You bought this book since you tried everything to become healthy and maybe you lost the extra pounds here and there, but found yourself regaining it right back. You were determined at one point when you tried that new diet and exercise routine, but somewhere along the way you lost the fortitude and went back to your previous routine. This book is about getting off that diet rollercoaster, which is actually harming your good health, and getting onto a lifestyle change that will bring years to your life.

The journey, no matter how long it takes, will help you lose up to a pound a month, which equates to 12 pounds a year, 24 pounds in two and 48 pounds in four. If you think losing a pound a month is too slow, then think about how gaining one pound a month from this day forward would look like. If today is your 40th birthday and you weigh 190 pounds and you gain a pound a month, you would be 250 pounds by the time you are 45. If you continue on, you would be 540 pounds when you reach age 70. Okay, not exact science but you get the point. I will go as far as to say that even losing a half a pound a month is pretty substantial melting 30 pounds of body fat in five years.

The law of compounding is based on what you do each day repetitively that can either work against you or work for you. The law that you applied throughout the years that got you to this unhealthy state will be the same law that will get you out of it. The reason why gaining weight is much easier to achieve is because television, sweets, and pizza gives you immediate mental and physical pleasure, while losing weight instills a recall of sacrifice and displeasure. Let's remove the negative stigma locked deep in your mind and use the same compounding effect to become what you envision to be your ideal healthy body. More important, the journey can be simple and enjoyable if you change the perception simply by working smarter by maximizing time with effective and efficient effort. To accomplish this, you must put health back in the forefront and make it your primary focus above all else.

Focus and putting health at the forefront means to draw your undivided attention to it and heighten your awareness to all things health. That in itself will naturally manifest your state of mind to making health and fitness a top priority. I'm not saying to neglect all other things that are important in life but reposition the focus to the top of your list so to avoid waking up five years from now at 250 pounds. There is a higher sense of awareness where you begin to notice related things that where there all along when you focus on it which you never even noticed before. That is what we need to achieve with focus and forefront when it comes to health and fitness at this stage of life. So what I explain and the mental action items we will perform will require this higher level of focus thus making it the forefront of importance.

This process is very simple and requires you to think about the subject of health at all times. There will not be any physical action on your part, but the mental act of recognizing anything health related throughout your day. When you are in a crowd, take a moment to notice those who are overweight versus those who are fit. When you read your morning news about politics and finance, first flip or scroll to the health and fitness section and glance at a few articles. If something catches your eye, read it so to put that above finance, sports, or the wrong doings of others. Another focus and forefront exercise is to notice the person taking that morning or evening jog or that couple you blindly noticed doing their routine walk. The idea is to seek out and begin to focus on all things health so you begin noticing all those invisible things you never paid attention to, forcing it to the forefront of your consciousness. Practice this exercise from this point forward and begin to condition yourself. Although it may seem trivial and perhaps silly, this effort only takes a fraction of a second yet is extremely effective.

What heighten my focus even higher during my personal journey was when I began to read articles about various health conditions and illnesses of other people. I began to notice that there was always the theme of prevention in these informative pieces. Diseases such as colon cancer, heart disease, stroke, diabetes, breast cancer, kidney cancer and several others are all aggravated by being overweight and sedentary. Take a look at the various sites and you will notice many illnesses mentioned can be prevented simply by applying weight control measures, increasing physical activity, and maintaining a proper diet.

Everything about health and fitness came to the forefront when I noticed that those who neglected any form of exercise and proper nutrition looked miserable and unhappy. I once overheard a distraught middle-aged women, sadly struggling with obesity, who was bound by her wheelchair complaining about the cost of her medications. Imagine travelling through life bound to a wheelchair and reliant upon a pharmacy. This woman will never know it, but she has left an indelible mark on my life—in a good way. Hence another reason to write this book hoping her and others will find their way here and transform to better health.

GOING FORWARD WITH MOMENTUM

Stop and think about how you feel about your current weight and health. Do you feel good about yourself? Do you feel guilty, helpless or stuck? Do those feelings offer you any affirmation, motivation, self-worth or enthusiasm? We've all been there and we tried. You know you should eat better and exercise, but that enthusiasm fades away and you blow it off until you are reminded when something triggers the thought. It is like you neglected to do the required car maintenance and kept putting if off until one day your car breaks down and you are stuck unable to move. When that day happens, you feel helpless and frustrated because you knew you had to take the time to do the scheduled maintenance. You begin to kick yourself for not taking action to make that appointment, set aside the time and take the necessary steps. Now the regret creeps into your thought, and you become overwhelmed with emotions of "should have" and "could of." Say somehow after numerous tries you get lucky and the car miraculously starts. You make a promise to yourself that you will get it fixed tomorrow. For the next several days, while neglecting your promise, each morning after several desperate attempts you still somehow get it to start and you continue to promise to fix it until it fades into normalcy. Then the inevitable day comes when the car completely dies—and at the worst possible time!

Essentially, at your current state of unhealthiness, you know you need to fix it and because you knowingly put it off, you are left with this feeling of uneasiness that one day the body will break down at the worst moment of your life. When you do nothing to prevent the predictable, there is a helpless feeling of regret that you will carry each and every day. Even though there will be unexpected illnesses as the body ages, if you act on doing something toward your health, at least you did the necessary standard maintenance to minimize the regret of neglect. If you take some action, any action be it big or small, those feelings of uneasiness and regret will no longer haunt you. Because you are in the mindset of always being progressive and doing something, it will no longer leave you with the uneasiness of getting stuck and helpless one day.

The power of progression is extremely important, as it offers a deep-rooted feeling of calmness and inner peace within the mind. When you begin to reap the rewards of progress, you begin to see a positive change as the mind naturally perpetuates self-momentum with lasting longevity. In essence, you are enjoying the journey from this point forward as you begin to shift your life to joy and happiness rather than pain and suffering.

When it comes to getting healthy and fit, you must be a participant and not a spectator. So at any time of the day when you are reminded about getting or staying healthy, you are left with a feeling of reassurance because you are doing something about it and not just surrendering and feeling overwhelmed. To continually sustain this level and enjoy the process is to always be moving forward to avoid hitting plateaus and becoming stagnant and bored. It will be an unlimited house you can build upon with no end to improvements in the pursuit of becoming healthy and fit forever. It takes a level or awareness of what is your current state, what needs to be changed, what actions needs to take place, and what needs to be completed and repeated to ensure you're constantly in motion.

MOTIVATION IS KEY

Everyone wants to be healthy and fit so you would think that would be enough to motivate you to start, continue and accomplish it. Yet only a fraction of people are healthy and fit and the rest are struggling to even begin. You try to convince yourself to get off the couch and stop eating an entire pizza with a pitcher of beer every Sunday, Monday and Thursday (go team!). Come the following day, you tell yourself that you will start tomorrow and when tomorrow comes you don't refrain and you tell yourself once again that you will start tomorrow. The motivation here is that eating pizza tastes so good especially with a pitcher of beer spending an entire Sunday buried in your favorite chair watching television (fun). The flip side to TV, beer and pizza is to eat a plate of vegetables with some water while doing the laundry and folding clothes for the rest of the day (boo).

You lost focus because you chose instant gratification as opposed to what needs to be done to avoid future distress. Becoming healthy and fit is an afterthought and although you know you should, the effects are not instantly apparent so there is no motivation to change. Just for the record, I am not anti-pizza and I have no issue with liquid barley. In fact, I eat my favorite deep-dish, Chicago-style pizza on special occasions. My point is that it is extremely hard to motivate yourself to get healthy and fit when the alternative is so much fun. What if after several years of doing the pizza thing, week after week, you feel a dull pain in your chest with an overwhelming feeling of nausea and fatigue? You get up to tell someone, but you trip over the empty pizza boxes and empty beer cans and blackout when you hit the floor. When you wake up, you find yourself in the hospital and the doctor tells you that you had a heart attack. You ask how to prevent this from happening again and he says, "If you don't take care of yourself you will probably have a massive heart attack one day soon."

While most people would be motivated to change after a life-threatening incident, some of us may not get a second chance. The reason I'm targeting those in middle age is because this is the time most of us realize we are not invincible and that life is a gift. I've experienced the emotional anguish of many of my friends who suddenly died from a heart attack or were diagnosed with Diabetes brought on by being overweight.

Becoming a father for the first time in my mid-forties motivated me to find the energy and stamina to be able to run and play with my son. I also didn't want him to be fatherless early on or see me whittle away year after year due to poor health. I wanted to give myself a fighting chance to go on camping trips, see my son graduate from college, be at his wedding, and hopefully, enjoy grandkids.

So what's your motivation to change? Here are some to help you get started on your journey:

- Cardiovascular disease, stroke and diabetes can be preventable diseases
- Looking and feeling younger than your biological age
- Do it for yourself to feel better about who you will become
- To have the energy throughout the day without feeling run down and out of breath
- To not be a slave to drugs just to function
- To avoid needing a walker or cane to get around
- To be mobile and free to go anywhere unassisted

Not resonating with any of the above? Then what about these family oriented motivators?

- To watch your kids grow up and thrive into adulthood
- To be able to spend your 401k after so many years of saving
- To be able to travel during your retirement years
- To be able to hold and play with your grandkids
- To grow old together with your significant other
- To not die in a nursing home or at a hospice facility

There is a voice in your head that is often called the resistance wall which for a split second will try its hardest to talk you out of proceeding. Often times when you are about to do something that requires a lot of work up front, we think about what is involved and how hard it will be.   Then for that split second, we become overwhelmed with the emotions of suffering, pain and sacrifice that only adds fuel to stop and quit. If you can only have the awareness and strength of pushing through that brief hurdle and ignore the voice and just do without thinking ahead of what we have to do, then it becomes easier to push forward. The simple technic to overcome the resistance wall requires you to be aware of when that voice of confrontation is trying to talk you out of what you need to do. When that voice starts talking, remind and recall the reason and purpose you listed as motivation. It will not be easy at first and that voice is relentless but I guarantee you will begin winning the battles as the voice will eventually fade away and stop altogether. There will be occasions when the voice will reappear but know it's happening and immediately push away the thoughts from entering my mind, ignore it altogether, and recall the reason and purpose of why you need to overcome is your line of defense. Find that personal reason that really hits home when you hit that split second wall of resistance and repeat it over and over again as I can promise you that the voice will become far and few between.

HABIT IS NOT A FOUR-LETTER WORD

The word "habit" gets a bad rap. It's almost always associated with something negative, when in fact, all successful people practice "good" habits. That's why they are successful. There are habits that are progressive in nature and help improve life mentally, physically and financially. Good habits usually require effort and are hard to do during the beginning stages, but become easier when they are repeated. I've put together a list of my own personal habits that help me move forward to strive to improve my health and overall being.

- Brushing and flossing my teeth after every meal
- Date night with my partner every Friday
- Reading a quality book every night like this one
- Listening and learning about self-improvement during my commute
- Frequently telling my family I love them
- Putting money into my retirement fund every pay
- Eating a solid breakfast every morning
- Getting seven to eight hours of sleep every night (Trying)
- Reciting five things I am grateful for every morning

Then there are habits of regressive nature that hurt and hinder you mentally, physically and financially that do absolutely nothing to improve your life. They have negative results that decrease your well-being as time moves forward. That one innocent day turned into two, three, four consecutive days fueled by either pleasure or satisfaction that eventually turns into months and then years. Now it turned into a bad habit that is next to impossible to break because you either enjoy it too much or it requires days to years of effort to reverse the process.

- Smoking cigarettes
- Drinking alcohol every night
- Watching the news before you sleep
- Cursing and getting angry about traffic during your commute
- Doing work on the weekends instead of spending time with your family
- Spending beyond your means and not saving for retirement
- Eating donuts every morning for breakfast (I love apple fritters)
- Getting four to five hours of sleep
- Thinking about all the things you hate about your job

Both sets of good and bad habits have the ability to last for years due to their compounding effects. Compounding effect means each time you do something repeatedly, and frequently, it adds to the prior day, snowballing until you stop and notice the desired or undesired results. If you stop and think about what you do every day from morning to night, then you will begin to notice that you have a pattern of doing them around the same time each and every day. When you wake up, you do the same morning ritual, take the same exact route to and from work, drink the same morning cup of coffee, eat lunch at a specific time, leave work on the hour, do your evening ritual of eating dinner, brush your teeth and go to bed (alright already). The repetition and consistency begins to brainwash you without the need to stop and think continuously every single day. It may have been challenging or perhaps rewarded you with pleasure at first, but because it works for you and you do it repetitively, it eventually becomes second nature without the need to think. You are ultimately creating a sense of comfort that gives you expected results for something you want to do and also something you have to do each day. In essence, it becomes a habit.

You will encounter throughout the journey two distinct actions for creating a new habit and at the same time altering an old one. Creating a new habit will be easier to do than changing an old one. A new habit is like building a house from the ground up. It is progressive in nature and if you continuously hammer the nail to the wood, it eventually gets built. To change a habit is like renovating a house—you have to work with what's already there. It involves more awareness and methodical thinking in order to successfully tear down and begin to shift the changes to your desired outcome and results.

Good and bad habits require a blueprint that must be simple to follow. Creating habits is the conditioning of the mind through repetitive action and is used by all successful—and unsuccessful--people. High achievers and low achievers condition themselves for success or failure through habits. I'm not trying to lecture you or tell you something you already know since I am sure you already know how and why you became out of shape. My goal is to help you change the traditional way of approaching how to become fit and healthy by focusing not on your glut and core, but working on your brain first in order to achieve success.

For most of us, our body is not stopping us from health and fitness achievement. Our minds are! Your mind tells you that there is pain and suffering involved in getting healthier, and that you have to sacrifice pleasure, time and money. This journey will help you shift your thoughts from being lost and helpless to being in total control of your health and fitness through short, easy and simple repetitive actions that can sustain longevity with no limitations.

You are going to condition your body by empowering your mind to first eliminate the traditional approach of sacrifice, time, pain, equipment, money or any excuse that has prevented you from achieving health and fitness in the past. The journey will show you how to create a habit within you to achieve your desired results using minimal effort and sacrifice.

Sounds like some kind of black magic but if you think about it, you became overweight with minimal effort and displeasure so why can't we do the same but for the opposite effect. There is a heavy emphasis on awareness and knowledge throughout the journey, which is one of the essential elements you will encounter that will lead you to achievement and sustainment. It is going to be an eye- opening experience that when you understand and master the essence of mental practice, you will become in control and unstoppable for the rest of your life.

STOP WASTING YOUR TIME

Did you know that spending hours on a treadmill day after day is actually bad for the aging process? Did you know that eating food labelled low fat is actually making you unhealthy? Were you aware that doing sit ups every day will not flatten your stomach and may make your waist appear bigger? Did you know that eating late at night has nothing to do with gaining weight? Attempting to stay healthy and fit is challenging in itself, but so many people who act upon the misinformation unfortunately waste their valuable time and effort not knowing why they are not seeing any improvements.

I, too, was part of that group of fitness warriors who spend hours at the gym but never see any significant results. The more I worked out, the less my physique changed. Frustrated, I decided to research anything and everything about exercise and nutrition to find out why this phenomenon was happening to me, as well as others. And I discovered I was doing everything I thought was right—wrong.

I wish I had known from the beginning I was making mistakes and bad choices that would hinder my fitness goals or at least slow them down. While I cannot edit my history, luckily I have the awareness and foresight to apply what I discovered in my 40s to my 50-something self today. I achieved my health and fitness goals just when I reached middle age and have been able to sustain them now for more than 15 years.

I wish someone hit me over the head early on and guided me on to how to think and how to view nutrition and exercise in such a way that was simple, realistic and effective. I have served my purpose if I can guide you and others on a more direct route to your fitness goals, saving you valuable time and money. This clear-cut awareness is simple and surprisingly easy to achieve. From this point on, and throughout the journey, I will challenge you to educate yourself on what is real and what is just smoke and mirrors.

One reason why most people have difficulty accomplishing their ideal health and fitness goals is because marketing makes it so confusing and complicated. Fitness isn't about getting there quickly or using a state-of-the-art piece of equipment or taking a pill that will solve all your weight problems. The fitness and food industries take advantage of our lack of knowledge about exercise and nutrition to sell yet another product that promises something it can't deliver. They hate people who are willing to read nutrition labels or look beyond the dramatic before-and-after photos to find out what it really took to get healthy and fit. My intention is not to list all the false claims, but to instill this awareness of what to look for and how to reprogram the way you educate yourself about nutrition and fitness.

What I want to share is a very simplistic view of food, nutrition and exercise that's supported by knowledge, facts and informed choices. The following is not a lesson on what foods have the most saturated fat, or the benefits of each of the alphabets of vitamins, or which new exercise routine you should do. The overall concept includes easy-to-follow fundamentals on how to discount the false or misguided claims that manipulate decisions and inadvertently promote, or increase the odds, of becoming even more overweight and unhealthy.

Getting healthy is not as simple as eating fewer calories, burning more fat through rigorous exercise or following the designer diet. As a matter of fact, I promote eating more because if you starve your body of food, then the body will resist by slowing down your ability to burn fat, making it even more difficult to lose weight. When your metabolism slows down, it is trying to protect itself from starvation by releasing a barrage of anti-defense weapons called hormones. At first it may seem like you are losing weight when you drastically cut back on your food intake, but in reality you are dangerously depleting water and cannibalizing valuable muscle, which is the most damaging effect. The body is designed to survive and it will do everything it can to stay alive. So if you starve it, it will slow down your metabolism to keep your energy supply as long as possible. And if you overfeed it, the body thinks you want to store the food for later use. The body has tremendous capacity to store excess fat for emergencies, but if that day never comes and you don't use it, then there is a tax on other parts of the body to carry and keep it. It's your body's survival mechanism that is adapted from our ancestors' evolutionary environment of feast or famine.

The simple equation is the total amount of calories you eat is either less than or greater than what you burn throughout the day. The type of food you eat to fulfill those calories will dictate how you feel during the day, thus effecting your quality of your life in the short and long run. Lastly, you need to know what movement maximizes the process of burning calories and improving the body for years to come.

So let me simplify the journey and explain the entire process in a few sentences.
- To achieve a healthy and ideal body, no matter how much and how long you exercise, food is 80% of the equation.
- In order to become fit, you need to do four focused movements, lasting two to three minutes, every day for the next 21 days.

- The only thing that's required on your part is an in depth awareness of being present to who you are and how you react to your life.

So be aware and knowledgeable about your current health and fitness status by scheduling an annual physical to get data that will help you establish a realistic baseline. As you move forward, that will be your indicator to monitor any changes in your vital signs. This is stepping up the self-awareness of how your health condition is today, what issues you may have, what consequences exist if not addressed and acknowledge changes to your state as you get older. Although this may not tell the whole story, it is a mental commitment that your health is important, and it is always something you will need to work on as we embark on this journey together.

CONSISTENCY IS THE REAL GOAL

You would think your goal is to get healthy and fit, but surprisingly, that is not the ultimate goal of the book. The goal here is simply to be consistent and create a habit of action. You've already tried to lose weight and eat healthier, but like most people (including myself), you couldn't sustain either one. You had good intentions, but it is a life-altering choice that realistically is a very large undertaking that requires laser-sharp focus. To reverse years and years of undesired habits will require much more than following a commercial diet program or joining a fitness club. In fact, these traditional measures will only get you more frustrated, disappointed and discouraged about attaining your fitness goals. I'm going to help you change your "old" way of thinking and embrace a mindful approach that is easier, smarter and more sustainable than anything you've ever done before.

My success hinged on a simple, but powerful, conscientious shift from the physical challenge to the mental challenge. I started to put more emphasis on the "habit" of getting healthier rather than on the "goal" of becoming more fit. The idea is that no matter what happens throughout your day, your habit of fitness is so strong that you don't alter it to fit your mood or circumstances, as both of those will constantly change. What you're trying to build here is fitness consistency on a mindful level.

To simplify things, like anything that seems overwhelming, this book breaks down the process of getting healthier into phases with time thresholds and milestones. You will be competing with only yourself and will learn to battle your inner conflict so you can overcome any hurdle or wall of mental blockades. There will be many moments during the journey that you will face a brick wall and at that moment you will need to decide whether it stops you or you stop it by picking up a proverbial sledgehammer. I need you to be aware so when that moment occurs you will be mentally prepared to recognize it and move forward instead of backwards. If you do not recognize it is happening, you will feel justified to give into excuses and stop, therefore never having the ability to break out of the unhealthy and unfit state you are in today.

During your journey, you will hit these barriers and if you are aware and recognize them as happening, regardless of the reasons, then you know to ignore that split-second voice of resistance and push through it. That millisecond "conquest" decision will change your life from being miserable and frustrated to being happy and unstoppable. In the past 15 years of my journey, every mental barrier I pushed through gave me more strength to tackle the next one. When my mother was undergoing chemotherapy treatments, when my father was recovering from a debilitating stroke, when my wife suffered a miscarriage and when my son was diagnosed with a learning disability—on and on the "excuse" barriers have come my way. I'm no different than you in terms of experiencing crippling emotional challenges. But what is different for me today is that I have developed the mental muscles I need to thwart the negative voices that are powered by life's difficulties. You can't change the randomness of life, but you can change how you react to it.

I'm still dealing with the after effects of those challenging moments presently the death of my mother, but I am pushing forward regardless so I can help others overcome the emotional barriers that will occasionally emerge throughout the journey. It is extremely important for you to be aware of any such obstacles because every single day from now on will require you to take action for 21 days without missing a day.

The action is to carve out two minutes each day for simple and quick exercise movements and do them until they become second nature. Overcoming the mental challenge each day will be a decision you will be faced throughout the journey and once you falter, you either start over or try again when you are ready. If you don't feel like doing the mental and physical actions that day, then reflect upon your personal motivation and use that to help you decide if you want to push your way through it. Remember that consistency is the goal and that getting healthy and fit is the byproduct of the repetitive act.

The challenge is that the rewards are not immediate and offer no immediate pleasure but expect a feeling of great accomplishment that you overcame the resistance. You will apply this to the decisions you make about what you eat and drink as you learn more and more about the impact nutrition has on your long-term health. The goal is to accomplish a daily achievement through consistency of doing one single behavior over and over again. As time progresses, the changes you continue to make will not be difficult as you will have already established consistency as the main motivator of your good health. For example, if the journey required you to tap your head three times right before you sleep every night for 21 days, then you will become so acclimated that failure to do so will cause uneasiness if you don't do it (for example only).

Those acts you will be doing to reach your habit goal is half of the equation. The other half will concentrate on breaking bad eating behaviors while carving out new ones simultaneously. My job is to make it simple, uncomplicated and interesting enough for you to follow along easily so to enjoy the journey throughout. If you have read the above mindset preparation and truly took the effort of envisioning, focusing, prioritizing, finding your motivation and know that this is no longer a choice but a requirement, then you are ready to begin the 21-day journey. All this mental preparation will be a waste of time if you do not have the blueprint needed to accomplish the goal of creating constructive habits.

When I started thinking about writing this book, the first thought that jumped into my head was the task was too daunting, too intimidating, too laborious for me to even consider. But I had a passion to help others who are searching for a proactive and effective way to combat the inevitable aging process. So I applied the same approach that you will use on your journey to mine. I began to envision the celebration of finishing the book. I tapped into my motivation of changing at least one person's life. I focused on writing at least one hour every day by putting consistency in the driver's seat. At first, it was challenging and often times I wanted to quit. However, by being aware of the negative voice in my head I was able to push it aside and move forward into action instead of retreating into inaction. The first step is awareness. The next is action. And during the journey, you will begin to shape your own method of counteraction and defense once you become intimate with your negative voice and overcome its temptation. Taking a new approach, fueled by self-care, will lead you closer and closer to your goal.

AWARENESS + GOAL x ACTION = SUCCESS

Lastly, awareness will get you started. A goal will cement what you're striving for and action is the key that starts your engine—literally. Combine all three and the only possible outcome is success. It's the law of the universe and you are part of it. The goal is to reprogram your thoughts to create a habit of consistent action until it becomes second nature. When the habit is instilled into your subconscious, similar to brushing your teeth or washing your hands, then getting things accomplished and reaching your objective becomes part of your day without hesitation and doubt. The purpose you defined as your motivation is key, but I will also add, that if you continue on until the end of the journey, you will enjoy a quality of life full of enthusiasm and zest.

You already know this, but why is it so difficult to take action and continue to do so for the rest of your life? I always use the analogy that life is faced with mountains to climb and how difficult it is to climb up and over it, but as you climb one, the next mountain will become easier to overcome. At any beginning when you are at the base of a steep mountain looking up, you feel overwhelmed as to how hard and how long it will take to climb to the top. First off, you have no clue as to how to accomplish this next to impossible task, let alone knowing how to start, how to keep going and how to reach the top. So you end up feeling so overwhelmed, discouraged and completely lost as to what to do. Then a rush of negative thoughts begin to talk you out of it, desperately trying to convince yourself of all the reasons you should stop and not even try. You begin to create excuses such as "It's too hard," "What if I get hurt," "It might rain," or anything else that will give you an out. Negative self-talk does absolutely nothing for you—except create a bad mental habit.

Successful people all have one thing in common: They didn't give up. When you look for excuses or you put something off until next year, you're allowing negative self-talk to control your choices. Free will? Forget about it. Negative self-talk sucks up so much energy and space in one's head that it's almost impossible to escape that dangerous neighborhood without a casualty. Make a conscience effort to reject the wasted thoughts of excuses and reasons that are preventing you from taking any action. Turn your mental radio to the progressive station and let it help you reach your desired outcome.

We all tend to look up at the top of the mountain instead of at the base where it all begins. You can take the mental leap you'll need to climb up high by creating an action plan that is carved out in definable, doable and daily steps. The most important aspect of an action plan is not the plan itself, but the action of doing what is on the plan and continuing on until you complete an accomplishment. To make it easier, I have created an action plan that is simple to follow, but requires tactful effort from start to finish. The principles that you apply will not only achieve a healthy and fit lifestyle, but will give you the blueprint to achieve anything you desire in life. Like anything new, the mind will constantly try to prevent and derail you from continuing, but you will combat that by having a plan designed to fight it and re-enforce your commitment through progressive actions.

I will be with you throughout the journey and support your efforts by reminding you of all the things you read earlier about focus, vision, purpose, awareness, motivation and progression. To instill a beneficial habit, action plus consistency needs to be applied. Period. The initial action you will be taking on your journey requires only two minutes to perform. You must engage in this action every night approximately one to two hours before you sleep. Your gym equipment is your bed and your gym clothes are your pajamas. The only skill you need is the ability to sit and stand. The efforts may seem trivial at first, but there is a psychological significance as to why they are short and easy to perform. I've observed trainers putting their clients through rigorous workouts that leave them totally exhausted and sore for days. The next time the client gets ready to go to his/her workout, flashbacks of pain, suffering and resistance often leaving a negative imprint that gets engrained deep in the subconscious. I take a different approach because this is a lifetime commitment and it's imperative you always think about the long run so there is no sense of urgency to get somewhere--fast.

You are striving to recondition your mind--through consistency--to change bad habits into productive choices. The actions must be taken in incremental steps so you gradually adapt to the new routine and it becomes rote in nature. If you miss a day, don't harp on it. Look at why you didn't participate in your well-being and acknowledge it. Then, move on to the next day. This is a pivotal moment of awareness, so it is extremely important to reflect on your choice of foregoing your health and fitness routine. If you miss two days in a row, then you hit the resistance barrier. It is extremely important that you reflect on your decision to skip day two, as this will help you leap over the "excuse" hurdle that is now in front of you. This awareness may seem like a small act, but it will pay off in huge dividends in the not-to-distant future. Whether you see it or not, you are starting to crush the "all-or-nothing" attitude that has kept you stuck for so many years. Awareness will allow you to recognize the emotions that stalled your efforts of consistency. Action will help you avoid them as you continue on your journey.

Lastly, the key to achieving habits is consistency so doing the act each and every day is an imperative must. You are programming a new pathway into your sub consciousness that will eventually become permanently engrained. Remember, half the battle of implementing an action plan is starting, so let's begin with baby steps forward. Keep in mind that progression creates momentum, which leads to motivation, which results in accomplishment. If you have fully absorbed everything discussed so far, and applied the mental preparedness discussed, then you are ready to begin.

Welcome to the start of your 21-day journey. It will teach you how to finally be in control of your choices and achieve health and fitness that will last a lifetime. One thing I need to mention. The day's talks will start off short and brief to be in in conjunction with easing into a paradigm shift but we will eventually ease in the progression and momentum as we begin to deep dive as we get closer to the end of our journey together. Now, let's get moving.

PART II
Your Journey. Your Program. Your Achievement

First off, I want to thank you for entrusting me to take this journey with you and giving me the opportunity to share my experience with you. In order to achieve your lifelong goal, it's critical that I follow along throughout the process to help re-enforce your new mindset and explain the emotional challenges.

The following actions will be performed every night before you go to sleep for the purpose of becoming and staying fit forever. It is simple to do without any real physical demands and can be completed in less than two minutes. The action may seem inconsequential at first but stay with me throughout as it will have a profound impact both your mind and body.

Since you are close to 40 years in age (lucky you) or older, the beginning phases are what I refer to as the "Wax On, Wax Off" stage. It is extremely critical to follow along to master the technic. The daily journey will alter your behavior by increasing your awareness of how food reacts in your body. When you reach day 21, you'll not only discover how mentally strong you are, but you will have created a mind/body connection that can never be deprogrammed. So regardless of the degree of where you are both mentally and physically at the end of the book, you will gain the knowledge to reach your goals going forward.

At the end of the journey, if you feel you haven't reached your goal of creating and reprogramming yourself or you want to continue further to maximize your full potential, I have that covered, too. There will be another journey waiting for you to embark upon if you so choose to deepen your knowledge of the body/mind connection. Remember, my purpose is for you to learn and become healthy and fit forever, so I will be with you to help you until you reach your destination.

🏋 Look for this symbol which means you must perform the movements that will be described in the following instructions.

CAUTION
Always consult a qualified medical professional before beginning any nutritional or exercise program. The exercises, movements, and nutritional suggestions are not intended to substitute for proper medical advice.

Enjoy the adventure. It will change your life forever. I promise.

DAY 1
STARTING IS HALF THE BATTLE

If you think way back to your college days, just starting a research paper was more of a challenge than writing it. You would put it off and find any excuse to delay it until you reach a point where you have no choice but to buckle down and begin. Once you get going and overcome the procrastination, momentum soon after writing down your first sentence, you were able to work feverously until you finally finish the night before. When it comes to your health, you don't want to wait until you have no choice but to start now because there are no extensions or makeup exams in life. The only equipment you will need to kick off this phase is a bed and your willingness to begin. You will be doing four separate moves, five times each, every night before you go to bed. By day seven, the movements will feel natural and comfortable, which means your mind and body have adapted to the routine. To avoid becoming complacent and keep momentum and progression going, you will make slight adjustments in the movements while easing into the next transition.

Seven days thereafter, the body and mind will adapt and you will continually add to the movements until you reach the 21st day. The movements will remain easy and simple and will never exceed more than four minutes to complete. You are already an expert on form and techniques since you do these moves naturally throughout your daily grind. It is extremely important to follow and focus on the breathing instructions and make sure that the movements are performed smoothly, slowly and steadily. My 91-year-old father is able to do this routine with ease. I suspect you will be able to do them, too! Both written and video instructions are available to ensure that you understand how to do the movements correctly.

QRCode Help:

Apple™: https://support.apple.com/en-us/HT208843
Android™: https://www.wikihow.tech/Scan-QR-Codes-on-Android

Full Video:
http://hff.passionhabit.com/exersize-and-equipment/

Move One – Sit Down and Stand Up

Stand next to your bed facing outwards with your back legs shoulder width apart and against the frame. Now sit down on your bed while inhaling.   As soon as your "back side" (butt) barely touches the mattress, pause and slowly stand up straight while exhaling out. Do this move five times at a slow and even pace. Are you thinking this is too easy? Great, this is what I want you to feel. 🏋️

Video:http://hff.passionhabit.com/exersize-and-equipment/squat/

Move Two – Touch Your Toes then Stand Up and Look Up

Again, stand next to your bed facing outwards with the back of your legs against the frame shoulder width apart. Now bend over slowly, with your legs slightly bent, and try to touch your toes. Go as far as you can keeping your back straight or slightly arched (opposite of hunched) while inhaling as you bend over. Next, straighten up into a standing position as you exhale. When you are upright, look up at the ceiling to complete the move. Do this action five times with a smooth and steady motion. 🏋

Video: http://hff.passionhabit.com/exersize-and-equipment/deadlift/

Move Three – Curl It and Up, Up and Away

Stand in the same starting position facing away from the bed with your back legs touching the frame and your arms by your side, palms forward. Keep your elbows close to your torso and do a curl simulating the act of lifting two buckets of water up to your shoulders while inhaling. Pause for a split second and then slowly reach for the sky, fist closed like superman does when flying. Now, exhale and reverse the process by lowering your arms up to the position when you held the buckets next to your shoulders. Then pause and lower your arms with your palms facing forward back to the starting position. Repeat five times, inhaling at the start and exhaling as you descend from the top. 🏋

Video: http://hff.passionhabit.com/exersize-and-equipment/curlmilitarypress/

Move Four –Bed Pushups

Stand facing your bed with your legs slightly apart. Using the edge of the mattress as your support, slowly lower your body down as far as it feels comfortable to you. Exhale on the way down and inhale on the way up. Keep your back straight as you lower down and hover your nose right above the bed when you reach it. Then, push up. Perform five steady and slow pushups to complete your exercises for the evening. If leaning down onto the edge of the mattress is strenuous or have physical limitations preventing you from doing this movement, face a wall with your feet about 12 inches away from the wall. Keep your legs shoulder width apart and simulate a pushup while standing erect. 🏋️

Video: http://hff.passionhabit.com/exersize-and-equipment/pushup/

Half Way There

For most, that may have been easy. Too easy perhaps. For others, a bit challenging. Regardless of the ease or difficulty you experienced, you just completed the first hurdle—getting started. Simple and easy at the beginning stages is structured by design to condition the mind to accept and keep going. Embrace and dwell upon the emotion of accomplishment and feel excited that you are on the road to success. The next step is to do it again tomorrow night. I cannot stress enough the importance of consistency in your journey towards a healthier you. The only thing you need to do to reach what you envision as the ideal body is to come back tomorrow and review the moves and perform them once again. Although today was short and less of a challenge physically, remember that we are working on conditioning your behavior.   Each day, we will methodically chip away into your subconscious by engaging these simple moves to instill familiarity while applying moderate progression as the mind adjusts.

A similar example would be to change your circadian rhythm to wake up an hour earlier each morning by gradually going to bed an hour sooner. Rather than trying to brute force yourself to give up the hour, slow transitioning by incrementally subtracting 10 minutes each week for six weeks is palatable. The challenge is not necessarily waking up on time but behaviorally getting yourself to go to bed earlier.   It is a paradigm shift that impacts your daily schedule from changing your nightly routine to trying to getting yourself to fall asleep.

Making a lifestyle change is undoubtedly a challenge as most will find it a daunting task. Breaking any behavior that took years to condition will require a similar approach to reverse engineer and slowly rebuild incrementally toward a dramatic change. Not only will this apply for the four moves each night but also the daily behavior adjustments regarding food choices and obtaining nutritional awareness. More to come. Have faith in the process and trust me that everything will make sense and fall into place as we eventually reach day 21.

May I ask for one last favor before you go to sleep? Very important. When you wake up in the morning, reflect upon what you have accomplished and be proud that you are taking action to improve your health and fitness. It's a new day and a new life. Congratulations on embarking on this journey and be sure to meet me at the same time tomorrow night so we can continue on toward a life-changing pursuit. It is imperative that you stop at this point of the book and not race ahead. This is a step-by-step journey that builds upon one day to the next. Jumping ahead will not get you to the finish line faster—or in better shape! So on that note, good night and enjoy the rest of the evening.

DAY 2
COMPOUNDING and AWARENESS

I'm overjoyed but not surprised that you returned because it means you are focused and committed to changing your life. Please go back and review the moves below to begin auto programming the mind to deep root how and what to do.

Video:
http://hff.passionhabit.com/exersize-and-equipment/
Disregard the Equipment section and beyond as we will address it later.

The mechanics is the foundation for proper movement, so pay close attention on technique, breathing and pace. In a few days, you'll know the moves without referencing the instructions as you are training the brain to instill and adapt. That is the beginning stage of conditioning the mind and a glimpse into the premise of creating a new pathway in the brain to achieve a successful outcome.

Sounds like the simple act of memorizing, but it really is the basis of creating a constructive and perpetual habit. With that in mind, let's do the four moves right now if you haven't already done so. Let's give it a try. 🙆

Easy right? Day two is a pivotal because you have now started the compounding effect of placing one brick on top of another and building a strong foundation. At our age when we look in the mirror and notice another white hair or a wrinkle that just appeared, we begin to look at time quickly passing as a negative occurrence. If you flip that adverse thought, there are actions you can take where the passing of time can be used to your advantage to build upon a positive outcome. Such occurrences are dividends, interest earned, retirement fund, learning a new skill through practice and experience, and in your case, the daily habit of thought and action to become healthy and fit.

Today, day two, is significant because you have overcome 50% of the challenge of simply getting started. You have triggered the law of compounding by adding a second day to your fitness routine. You are now using the passing of time to get that much closer to the body you envisioned.

I want to request a favor once again to do a simple awareness exercise throughout the day. The mental exercise is not complicated and requires zero physical effort with minimal time needed, but the action is significant and vitally important to do. Starting tomorrow, take a mental note of everything you eat that is white in color, especially anything that is made or contains white sugar. Note in your head (or if you prefer to write it down) all the WHITE foods you ate during the day such as white rice, white bread, white pasta and so on. I will explain later as to why the color is noteworthy but for now, let's concentrate on just this single identifiable characteristic.

Additionally, take a 5 second moment to read the nutritional facts labels found on soda cans, dessert packages and snacks and look for any product that contains greater than 9 grams of sugar. This is a simple method of quickly identifying what products to reconsider when making your food choices. Also, focus on processed white foods, not to be confused with the obviously healthy ones such as egg whites, cottage cheese or plain yogurt, for example. I'm not asking you to drastically change your diet. I'm only asking you to begin the process of becoming aware of your current diet which "awareness" is key to improve and change for the better everything that matters in life.

Once you identify what and how much of it you consume, we will use this knowledge as a baseline to start. The premise behind this mental notation is to be conscious of your actions so to begin the behavior adjustment shifting the control of food instead of food controlling you. You will be surprised as to how much of it (white) we eat daily, so the intention is to change your perspective and appreciation about food eventually. So, when you eat your breakfast, lunch and dinner and everything in between, take a mental awareness inventory of everything you eat. Nothing more. I listed a free food counter app that you can download toward the bottom of the "**Exercise and Equipment**" web page if you prefer a systematic approach. I'm not suggesting to use the app to count calories but simply an alternative to writing it down or trying to recall what you ate throughout the day. That's all you need to do for now just to get your brain to wake up.

Lastly, tomorrow morning, reflect upon your efforts thus far and feel the positive emotions of accomplishment that you are participating in your own success story. I'm sure you are excited to read on or feel that what you read and did was short and not impactful. But I encourage you to refrain from doing so. I know you want to know who shot J.R. but it's imperative to stop here. The discussions will be short and sweet at the beginning days to ease into this life-changing event but stick with me as the process will all make sense as we go further along. Have a wonderful night and a productive day tomorrow. Good night.

DAY 3
WAX ON, WAX OFF

So proud that you are back for day three of your journey. Just showing up today is another small step toward improving your life. On this day, it still feels odd to get ourselves to start and do the four moves but remind yourself that it takes only a few minutes of your life and it is really easy to do. So on that note, let's get started by doing the four moves, five times each as shown on the videos and follow the breathing instructions. 🏌️

I am done and it actually feels good to get the blood flowing and feel the body temperature rise a bit. Your body is already telling you that energy is being spent. As simple and insignificant as the moves may appear to be, it is important to note that it is similar to adding another brick to your foundation. I call day three "Wax On, Wax Off" because you may question how these four easy and quick two-minute moves can be effective toward achieving a fit and healthy body.

Why "Wax On, Wax Off?" It refers to a movie where the student questions the teacher on how sanding and waxing can help him be a better person. The teacher shows him how repetition creates habit by instilling the movement within the subconscious mind for a bigger purpose. Without being too technical, in essence, he is re-wiring his brain to drill the moves deep into the mind and condition himself to react automatically without effort. At this stage of the journey, you are trying to get your mind to remove the uncomfortable thoughts of doing something you have never done before. Once the moves can be remembered without referencing and the actions become routine, then it is time to progress forward with a slight incremental change.

The body and mind can adjust to any demand and condition through practice and repetition.

I mentioned the importance of awareness and asked you to make a mental inventory of everything you ate throughout the day that was either white or contains white refined sugar. Let me briefly explain why the color white is so important so you are aware why I chose this simplified approach. All white and brown foods including table sugar is a carbohydrate. Carbohydrates are foods that eventually turn into sugar (glucose) when digested and released into your blood. The body needs sugar to function supplying an energy source but its delivery, what kind, and how much is key to good health. White foods as opposed to brown converts into sugar quicker and enter the bloodstream faster. So fast that the body cannot keep up and is unable to use and burn efficiently. The body wants to keep the excess sugar, so it stores it in storage typically in places where fat cells are abundant like your butt and gut. Later, I will explain the details about the difference and issues surrounding the conversion process including a way to measure the various white and brown foods (Glycemic Index & Insulin Resistance). For now, let's keep it simple and stay with the white food and refined table sugar identifier. More to come.

Hopefully you had the chance to do the exercise and if not, let's try to do a recall right now. Let me start. I had two teaspoons of sugar in my coffee this morning. Ate two pieces of white toast with my breakfast sandwich. Had some white noodles with my spaghetti for lunch. Had some white rice with my dinner and ate four Oreo cookies for dessert. How about you? I purposely ate without thinking today to illustrate how much sugar can easily be ingested if we don't think about our choices. Unless you are a marathon runner or some kind of athlete, you will never need that amount of sugar for energy and stamina. Unfortunately, we are not bears that hibernate for three months and need to store massive amount of calories to survive a long, harsh winter. We only need a fraction of what we eat daily (dang).

I like sushi, donuts and pizza so I'm not asking you to stop eating white and sugary foods, but instead, become aware of just how much of it you eat. For example, if you eat three slices of pizza every Wednesday during happy hour and notice you are slowly gaining weight, then eat two slices instead to stop the compounding effect. Your awareness becomes a tool to determine how much weight you want to gain, keep or lose. In other words, if you want to gain weight, eat three slices. If you want to maintain your weight, eat two slices instead. If you want to lose a little weight, eat one piece. And if you want to shed even more, eat a slice and forego the crust. That applies to all the white and sugary foods you eat repeatedly each day. If you use this simple method throughout, then you are in control of determining how fast you want to achieve that envisioned fit and healthy body. Incidentally, the sausage, pepperoni, tomato sauce and cheese toppings on the pizza are not causing your butt and gut to grow bigger. It's the crust. Think thin crust and or order Honey Wheat with Whole Grain Crust, which is offered at many major restaurant chains.   Just food for thought (oh no).

Tomorrow once again, make a mental note of everything you eat throughout the day that is white or contains sugar. This time, think about the frequency and pattern in your food choices. I'll expand upon it tomorrow night. For tonight, get some rest so you have plenty of energy for the challenges ahead. Sleep tight.

DAY 4
REVERSE THE POWER OF CONSISTENCY

I am truly and honestly glad that you are here with me tonight because it means another notch on your belt toward achieving your goal. You see, the difference between people who achieve success versus those who don't can be summed up in three words: incremental repetitive actions. On that note, let's do the four moves so you can be part of the success group by simply doing. Meet you back here so let's do it. 🏋️

I hope you remembered to breathe in on the way down and breathe out on the way up. Just be really careful and stop and sit down immediately if you begin to feel dizzy. It's not a race so take your time and breathe slowly on the way up and never hold your breathe. On day four, you either memorized the moves or are close to recalling how to do the four moves without reference. That is significant because it is the basis of creating a new habit through repetition and consistency. Once you can do the moves and the proper breathing without the need to think about what and how, then you have adapted.

Hopefully, you are aware of the white and/or sugar-laden foods you consumed today. Let me go first. I had hash browns, eggs and sausage for breakfast, one teaspoon of sugar and cream in my coffee, potato salad with ham for lunch, spaghetti for dinner and a late-night sandwich. It's easy to eat a variety of white foods throughout the day without even noticing. Awareness gives you accountability because you are cognizant of it. If you notice, I consciously only put one teaspoon of sugar in my coffee instead of my usual two. That's because I was aware that I usually put two, which was revealed through my mental list I did yesterday. Of course it was not impactful toward losing weight, but it was something I was not aware I did every day. Because I took the action to make a mental note of it, and I am now aware, I was able to make a behavioral adjustment regardless of the lack of impact. I am in control as opposed to blindly doing what I did for years without notice.

While consistency can be used to your advantage, it can also be detrimental. For example, the extra pounds you gained throughout the years was not caused by that one chocolate cake you ate or the whole pizza you devoured during your annual football party (fav sport). Weight gain, like weight loss, happens over a period of time. Become cognizant of your eating patterns and you'll be empowered to change them (I know already!). There's a reason it's called the "middle-age waistline" and that's because it took time to grow wider and thicker.

The difference for you is that you are now doing something about it by developing a mental list of what you eat consistently every day. So tomorrow, let's add to the mental list of awareness by including the type of liquids you consume daily. Your morning coffee, afternoon soda and dinner wine. Again, I'm not asking you to stop, but simply to look for those repetitive drinking patterns just so you become aware. It is extremely important to do this mental exercise as you will use it again as a tool to be in control of your habits. Have a wonderful night, kiss those you love and we'll meet tomorrow night.

DAY 5
AVOID BUILDING A WALL

Wow, you're on day five so let me give you a "high" five (get it, high 5 on day 5, sorry!). But seriously, congratulations for your commitment to your good health.

At this point, some people may begin to wonder off a bit as their negative subconscious mind urges them to return to their previously comfortable life of not taking action. That is called the wall, the hurdle, or what I often heard as the terror barrier. When people hit this obstacle, they have two choices: stop or push through. So are you going to quit or do the four moves right now? Avoid being the 95% that decide to do nothing and let's get moving. I'll meet you back in less than two minutes after I too will be doing the four moves with you.
💪

Great, you moved forward instead of backwards. Don't you feel good that doing what took only a few minutes pushed you over the hump toward success? This is huge because if you didn't join me and decide to quit, then our journey would have ended (sad face). Take a moment to enjoy the emotion of success and look forward to that body you envisioned in your mind. Ready?

Let me remind you of the profound reasons and purpose for being on this journey. At your stage of life right now, you have probably heard about or experienced the sadness of someone you know and admired that has been taken away. I had a friend that never took this journey you are on and while on vacation had a massive heart attack and died instantly. It broke my heart, as he had three beautiful young sons, a loving home and a wonderful and caring wife. I had a co-worker who was the nicest person you would ever meet, but had the worst eating and drinking habits. He ignored his doctor's advice and developed diabetes, yet he didn't take any action to circumvent his condition. The diabetes progressed and he had to have his feet amputated due to gangrene. His quality of life diminished dramatically as he was faced with pain and suffering on a daily basis. Soon after his surgery, he died. It's that hard to overcome and even harder if you are not mentally prepared especially without help. I still think about him till this day.

I'm sure you've experienced similar stories or heard about famous people such as legendary entertainers, gifted comedians and angels of music, who struggled to find their way out and lived a life full of medical challenges. On the flip side, there are those who have decided to take a similar journey you and I are on including former Presidents, several famous actors, media personnel and successful sitcom stars, to name a few. Many argue that no matter how much you exercise or how carefully you eat, you cannot avoid a heart disease if you are genetically predisposed. Yes, that is arguably true, but if you compound it with an unhealthy lifestyle, you're unnecessarily increasing your risk factors for disease. According to the New England Journal of Medicine, "among participants at high genetic risk, a favorable lifestyle was associated with a nearly 50% lower relative risk of coronary artery disease than was an unfavorable lifestyle." In other words, if you don't take action regardless, you are increasing the odds exponentially. Okay, with the fear factor out of the way, my point is that fear can be a good thing if it sparks positive action.

Before we end the night together, I want to chat about the mental food list we compiled throughout the day. I want to digress a bit so I can illustrate how this mental exercise helped me shed 30 pounds and keep it off for 15 years. When I was making this mental note for the first time, I became aware how frequent I drank soda. Every meal I would drink a can of soda and one before I went to sleep. I did an additional awareness exercise by finding out how much white sugar was added and found out that there is approximately 26 packets of sugar in each can of soda. I tried to quit cold turkey, but I loved soda so much that it was impossible to stop since it was a deep-rooted habit that was developed over many years. I slowly reversed the process by convincing myself that I could save $4 a day if I just drank water during lunch and focused on that one commitment. It took several attempts, but I was able to finally apply the principles of focus, awareness and action. I eventually drank water instead of soda during lunch and once that was achieved, I became in control of my behavior drinking. I also lost a lot of body fat from that point forward and created a new healthy habit that has benefitted my digestion, curbed my appetite and kept me looking young and healthy. I've replaced the night soda with a refreshing diet soda (what?), but I'm working on stopping that habit, too. Tomorrow I'll explain a simple change you can do that will help shrink your butt and gut.

Enjoy your night once again and I wish for you a deep and uninterrupted sleep. Good night and sweet dreams.

DAY 6
WHY OH WHY

Good evening. Since you're here with me tonight that clearly means you are on the cusp of making this a new habit. What is actually happening is the creation of a new pathway, and the rewiring of your brain to learn a skill through repetition of doing the four moves every day. When it becomes second nature, you'll have created a brand-new neurological wire. So it is extremely important that you continue to take action that will add to the process and enhance the way you think and feel. With that said, let's do the four moves now. No need to hurry. I'll wait for you to finish. 🏋️

Wasn't that easy like Sunday morning? I think it's time I let you in on a little secret as to why you are doing those four particular moves each night. Yes, you are creating a new habit, but these four simple moves have a purpose beyond repetition. After 10 years of doing everything wrong, and eventually studying the topic for a decade, I finally narrowed down what is the most effective and efficient way to exercise. In the bodybuilding world it is known as compound-resistance, weight-lifting training. Compound weight lifting is a method that targets multiple areas of the body at the same time, often referred to as a full-body workout. Targeting the entire body is essential because people over 35 who unexpectedly make sudden movements are putting demands on muscles they infrequently use. Surprise movements can negatively impact muscle, tendons and nerves causing pain and injury. This is even more prevalent as people age and become more sedentary. Without regular exercise, the muscles that keep us balanced and stable will get weak from atrophy. To avoid this, movement is a must.

You are becoming equipped both mentally and physically for the rest of your life with the knowledge—and power—you need to grow older in a healthy, vital capacity. So just keep in mind throughout your journey that there is a purpose and a reason for doing what you are doing. You may not see it on the outside, but your body is benefitting from it on the inside.

Last night I asked you to make a mental note of everything you ate that's white and sugary and challenged you to observe when and how often you consumed these foods. Is there something you eat or drink at the same time every day? Is it that cup of coffee every morning, a donut or a Danish, a candy bar for a snack or a favorite dessert after an evening meal? As mentioned over and over and over again (stop already!), it's critical to become aware of your unhealthy food patterns. Being aware of them is half the battle and the other half is reversing the process by using the same principle of repetitiveness to break the cycle. Like my awareness rant.

It will be challenging and will take several attempts to truly change an ingrained food pattern. Much like my former soda habit, breaking the pattern doesn't mean stopping cold turkey. It's a matter of finding healthier substitutes or slowly dwindling down the amount. Here is a substitution trick you can use that's practical and easy to remember. Every white food you eat has a brown alternative, so simply try to switch them out on a regular basis

(You can access some examples here: http://hff.passionhabit.com/food-replacement/).

If you eat white bread with your sandwich or hamburger, replace it with 100% whole wheat/grain bread or if you eat potatoes then replace it with sweet potatoes. Don't eat a veggie burger, it's not a real burger but a cheap knockoff. Sorry, got off topic. Anyway, if you eat white rice with your meals, replace it with brown rice and replace white pasta with 100% whole wheat/grain pasta. Don't worry so much about the amount of calories or how you eat at this point. The reason why I stress the brown alternative is because it is a low glycemic-index alternative, which means the body (liver) releases sugar slower into your blood thus keeping you fuller longer while stabilizing your blood sugar level. This is not an attempt to convert or make drastic changes but purely an awareness exercise that leads to a behavior modification.

As for the sugary beverages and foods you consume, look at the frequency of how often you're eating/drinking them and then consider making just one healthier alternative replacement. Just only one for now.

To sum it up, make a mental note of what you eat that is white and think about replacing it with a brown alternative. Consider the liquids you consume and think about how you can substitute them with something more beneficial to your body. This will not happen overnight, but if you continue to remain focused on it, you will chip away at an old habit only to create a new, better one.

We'll regroup tomorrow and see how the day went, as I'm working on my remaining patterns, too, and will be applying the principles discussed so far. Be sure to return because like learning math, what you learn today is another stepping stone for tomorrow.

Here is a tip I want to leave you with tonight: Try not to watch the news before you go to sleep, because according to recent scientific studies, it can have a negative impact on the quality of your resting behavior. Instead, think about three things that you are grateful for such as your family, your commitment to good health and the opportunity to make tomorrow better than today. Have a good night.

DAY 7
COMMIT OR QUIT

Today is day seven which means you're at the one-week milestone. It is vitally important that you stay on track from this point forward because one missed day easily turns into two, three, six, a year and eventually never. So I'm giving you this opportunity to pause now, return the book and come back when you are ready. I will still donate the proceeds to children in need, but I want to make sure you are truly ready and committed to take charge of your life and achieve your goal.

If you decide to stop, then you're not ready to make this a priority right now, which I can completely sympathize and understand. But if you decide to continue, then you will change your life in so many ways. The principles and laws that you will discover throughout your journey will reveal so many wonderful things about yourself that will open the doors for other achievements beyond health and fitness. As far as your target goal, think about what the results will be as you move further along. You will be so grateful that you found the strength to continue, and I promise when you reflect back, you will know it was one of the best decisions you ever made. You will have confidence, look terrific, have more energy, be healthier, and when the time comes, you will be able to run around with your grandkids.

So I'll give you a moment to decide right now if you want to stop and return the book or continue on your journey.

If you are reading this, I am so happy you decided to continue and that you are committed to taking charge and changing your life for the better. Even though I have reached middle age, the simple concept of cause and effect still blows my mind. The concept of "If you do nothing, nothing happens, but if you do something, something happens" still astonishes me because it is so simple, yet seems so surreal and unfathomable (whoa deep, dude!).

On that note, let's do something and make things happen. I spoke earlier about progression because the body adapts once it is conditioned, so I would like to change it up slightly. Instead of five times for each move, let's add three more so to make it eight times for each move. Before you start, make sure you breathe in through your nose at the starting position and breathe out through your mouth when you exert your energy. If you get light headed, especially when touch your toes and stand up, then stop, get your equilibrium back and try again--but slower. Also, when you do the bed push up, try to get up to eight, but if you find it difficult, do as much as you can until you begin to adapt. If using a bed is challenging due to a limitation, please feel free to use the wall instead if or when you are able to do so. Let's do it, and I will meet you back here soon. 🏋️

Now let's talk about food again. Hopefully, you are continuing to replace white and sugary foods with alternatives that are brown, such as choosing brown rice over white rice or wheat bread over white. Today, I had a breakfast burrito but did something different this time when I ordered. Because I had the awareness that the burrito would be wrapped in a white flour tortilla, I asked for a wheat alternative. The single act of replacing enriched flour with wheat is not only a behavior change, but doing something different that is confusing the brain. Often times, brown alternative foods may not make a big difference due to added ingredients such as High Fructose Corn Syrup (or not) but again, it is the practice of consciously making an alternative food selection other than your previous ways. When combining that with the four moves every night, you are doing something instead of nothing, altering your mindset to act and think "healthy".

So continue to look for ways to replace white with brown when ordering or cooking, and tomorrow I'll explain why the word diet should not mean sacrifice. Before we depart for the night, take a moment to think about all the things you are thankful for and really dig deep and feel the emotions. Before I sleep, I think of all the new things my son discovers and the gift of seeing the expressions of amazement on his face. It puts a silly smile on my face and a rush of happy emotions engulf my body, leaving me with so much gratitude that I'm alive to experience it. I can't wait to see him in the morning. Let's end the day on a happy note and look forward to tomorrow. Have a wonderful night.

DAY 8
A BODY OF HELPFUL INFORMATION

You came back, which means you are one day closer to your ultimate goal. It also means that you and I are part of the five percent of people who are doing something to improve their health and fitness. Be proud of what you've accomplished so far because you're beating the odds. Enough talking and more doing so let's take action and do this together right now and remember to do it eight times rather than five. 🏋️

I just finished, and adding three more reps to each move was a challenge, especially move one (sitting and standing) and move four (bed pushups). That extra effort is a gauge you can use to determine how many calories you need to burn to lose weight. Let me explain how the body works. When you challenge your body through these moves, you are actually making micro tears in your muscle fibers that will repair itself while you sleep and continue to do so throughout the following day. The body will look for energy sources needed to do the repair and rebuild by searching for fuel to use through calories. When energy food is depleted, it will turn to your butt and gut as its source. Each day as you do the four moves, the body begins to anticipate the stress and begins to protect itself by repairing the muscle fibers, but this time adding a small increase of muscle as insurance for future demand and stress. That additional muscle weight will require more energy to carry the load and again will use the overabundance of fast-digesting sugar found in white foods but when that source is depleted or replaced, it will turn to your butt and gut instead.

Brown foods work differently than their counter part. Rather than a free for all availability of sugar energy, brown foods are stingy to the body and release only small chunks at a time, so they have no choice but to take it from other energy sources. The reason why many people fail to become fit and healthy when it relates to food is because diet to them means eating less, to suffer and sacrifice. What diet really means is to eat enough to fuel your body to function accordingly without spilling over the excess into your body's fat cell storage areas like your hips and thighs.

Let's call it a night and continue to put health and fitness in the forefront. To help you focus, take a minute or two in the morning and read one brief article on health and fitness to start your day off with the proper mindset. Also, let's continue on with the awareness list of what things you eat that are white and sugary and look for things that you eat and drink repetitively every day at the same time. The latter is important to note because you will begin to notice behavior patterns that promote or hinder your health. Lastly, tomorrow night, I want to share some insight on food beyond what you now know about white and brown foods and explain why you shouldn't give up eating hamburgers, fried chicken and pizza (what?). So, as Juliet says to Romeo when saying goodnight, "parting is such Sweet sorrow." (Sweet! Get it. Bad!). The good news is that tomorrow is a brand- new day so let's recharge our batteries and once again be grateful that we can experience and look forward to another beautiful day. Sweet dreams (again with the Sweet?) and good night.

DAY 9
FOOD AS FUEL

Can you believe you reached day nine of your journey? You are clearly leaning on the side of "I will" instead of "will I" become healthy and fit. At this point, it may still feel new and somewhat uncomfortable, but think of it as playing the game of building a house of cards. Each card that you successfully add to the house is dependent upon the previous card, and the card after that eventually leads to a strong and solid foundation. Each day is critical as you add another card to your healthy body foundation. If you lose focus and place one bad card down, then you'll weaken your foundation. And if you stop altogether, then your house will never be built and eventually lead to falter like an abandon building.

Let's not waste any time or effort! Quickly do your four moves, eight times right now. After you come back, I will discuss why you should eat hamburgers, chips, pizzas and even hotdogs. So hurry back. 🏋️

I'm not sure if you experienced this, but for some reason, even though it was a bit more challenging, you probably feel comfort and fulfillment in the moves. That's your body combatting stress by replacing stress hormones (cortisol) with feelings of pleasure and reward (dopamine). If you haven't felt it yet, you will and you will know it. Your journey of reaching your goal of creating a habit is not just making your body healthy, but simultaneously, it's making your mind healthy as well.

It only gets better from this point forward, especially when you begin to see mental and physical progress. That progress will be filled with affirmation that will lead you to automatically motivate yourself to continue and improve. This auto-motivation will happen naturally without sacrifice or extreme mental stress because you are flipping what you felt as uncomfortable to what you are now physiologically enjoying. The enjoyment stems from the emotion of achievement and pride that you are in control of your body and not so much about how much weight you lost or how you look. Focusing on doing these four moves each day is conditioning the mind as the primary objective, while achieving a fit and healthy body is a secondary byproduct.

I mentioned earlier why you should continue to eat hamburgers, chips, pizzas and hotdogs and here is why. I'm not saying to go out and strictly eat these types of fun foods, but discuss why neglecting it will only make you crave and want it more. Like most people, I love eating hamburgers and french fries. In fact, I eat potato chips almost every day. I just polished off four slices of pizza at my son's birthday party two days ago, and I bought hotdogs fixings for dinner. True story and I have the receipts to prove it.

You see, eating these types of foods do not make you overweight, but the frequency of doing it will. I always say it is better to pick a random day once in a great while and binge on ice cream, soda, pizza and chips as long as you can control yourself the following day. To avoid getting technical and complicated, everyone has a limit on the amount of calories they can eat to maintain their current weight. If you eat beyond that limit, and add the fact that your metabolism is slowing down as you age, then the results are obvious. To prove my point, if you look around and notice those around you who are middle-aged and older, those who are fit and those who are not. I guarantee that most who are fit are those who work at it and make it a part of their daily life. We are talking fit not thin meaning proper food choices and some form of muscle resistance program.

So today, if you only eat junk food and limit it to that amount, technically you will maintain your current weight. But there is a catch. The catch is that you will feel terrible and uncomfortable. When you overeat during Thanksgiving or at a Las Vegas buffet, at the end of the meal you end up feeling bloated, uncomfortable, sleepy and lazy. That effects your mood and your behavior because when uncomfortable, you tend to become agitated and want to be left alone so you can take a nap. Instead of enjoying the family or going out to explore life, you want to be sedentary and let life pass you by.

Also, when you eat this way, you're like the crew on the Santa Maria slowly suffering from scurvy. Okay, maybe not scurvy, but some kind of deficiency. In other words, like your car, the engine needs certain additives to avoid clogging fuel lines, pipes and valves. Without these additives, your body's performance will slow down. It needs nutrient additives to help it flow smoothly and quickly, so you can perform and feel better. Metabolism is a key factor to a healthy and fit lifestyle. Here's a crude example of how powerful these additives can be. Have you ever had a bad case of junk-food constipation that ruined your day because you felt bloated, uncomfortable and just plain miserable? To circumvent the effects, you eat a bucket of prunes, truckload of oranges, a field of roughage, gallons of water and some shredded cardboard fiber mix. Soon after, you begin to flow like the Mississippi River, finally getting some relief and comfort. That's how much food can dictate your life from a world of suffering and discomfort to a life experience of happiness and spunk. The point of my rambling is that if you understand food and its effect on your body, it will explain why you get headaches, are always fatigued, and why you are always getting sick, depressed and tired.

The big mistake that people make to lose their butt and gut is to starve by cutting calories, but that would be a huge and unhealthy mistake.

That thinking and behavior will not work both mentally and biologically and is an unhealthy way of living. The body will adjust through hormones and slow down digestion (metabolism) because it feels and thinks you're starving. So when you go back to your previous eating habits, it will want to return to your former body and add more for insurance, making you worse off than before. Rather than cutting back and starving yourself, continue to eat the same amount of food, but change a few things here and there by substituting your choice of food.

I hope all this information sparked some food for thought (sorry for that). On that note, I want to wish you a wonderful sleep full of sweet thoughts and dreams. You deserve it. Let us connect tomorrow around the same time, as we will be going on a virtual trip on a tropical island to learn a valuable lesson on strategy and survival. Good night.

DAY 10
YOUR ISLAND PARADISE IS WAITING

Day 10 and you're almost to the two-week mark. At this point of the journey, you may feel some resistance as you are reaching a level of normalcy. That's a good thing because it means your mind and body is being challenged yet adapting. I bet my son's marbles that if you like the notion of accomplishment and feel it's making a difference, you are sure to reach your life-changing goal to be healthy and fit. So let's leap over the two-week barrier and get to it so you can add to your collection of efforts and achievement by doing four quick moves, eight times right now. See you back in two minutes. 🏋️

I was mistaken, it was less than two minutes because it's becoming easier as familiarity sets in. Now, without the need to recall the moves and doing them quicker, you begin to have this overwhelming feeling of calmness followed by the joy of triumph. Boy, that's a lot of sunshine.

As promised, let me share an interesting fact about using food as a tool by going on a journey that was supposed to be a two-hour island tour. Say we set sail from a port aboard a sightseeing boat, but the weather started getting rough and we get ship wrecked on a deserted tropical island. There are no cell phones, no LED lights, no hybrids or any other type of modern-day luxuries. Seriously, say you were on a deserted island off the grid and you had to find food to survive. One of the foods that you absolutely need to find is obviously water, as without it, you will die within 8 to 10 days from thirst and dehydration. The next thing you need is some kind of protein be it bugs, fish, a wild animal, eggs, or some plant combo. Without a steady stream of it, you will begin to feel fatigued, your body will start eating at your muscles, your hair and nails will fall out, you become anemic, depression sets in, and you will die within 70 days.

Another essential food group you absolutely need to find is fats. Not the fat we store in our butt and gut, but fats found in food. You look for foods like coconuts, seeds, nuts, and oils from fish, olives, and if you find an avocado tree, then you are set. When you eat fats, it actually keeps you feeling full. By the way, eating no fat can disrupt your hormone levels, weaken your bones and impair your digestion, because kidney problems and the immune function will eventually lead you to organ failure and death within six months. So eat your macadamia nuts, have that handful of peanuts, grab some pumpkin seeds, make that peanut-butter sandwich and order that big piece of salmon for dinner.

Yet another essential food that you need to find and eat would be fruits and vegetables. Without it, you will die from scurvy because you lack vitamin C causing gum bleeding while blood vessels begin to burst. You will become anemic with terrible stomach pain from digestive ailments such as constipation, hemorrhoids and diverticulosis, experience depression and confusion from vitamin deficiency, unable to see at night, become super weak with an irregular heartbeat from potassium deficiency. Beyond the nutritional need, they help move things along in your digestive system. You may not die immediately if you neglect fruits and vegetables, but you will feel terrible throughout the day, decreasing your quality of life mentally and physically.

You might notice one food group is missing from this desert-island survival menu. Did you guess it? Carbohydrates! That's because carbohydrates are not essential for survival.

When energy is not available in the form of glucose, then the body will look for other sources of energy found in protein, fat, and finally your butt and gut. Of course, another reason why you don't need carbohydrates is that fruits and vegetables naturally supply them with the added bonus of vitamins and minerals. I'm not suggesting in any way to cut carbohydrates altogether, because the brown alternative promotes healthy and smart weight loss. Bottom line, white carbohydrates and plain sugar is not needed as a source of glucose for energy. Real and essential foods will help move things along through your system, which increases metabolism, making you feel like a teenager in heat (ok, that's a stretch). With the added minerals and nutrients, you will feel light on your feet after a major bathroom accomplishment, giving you energy to explore life with enthusiasm and zest.

The simple message here is that you have choices and the tools to put you in control of how much you want to lose and when. If you want to lose a little, just change one thing from white to brown and if you want to lose a little more, change two things, and if you want to lose even more then change several more. The moral of our castaway story is that you are at the helm to cut out the white carbohydrates a little or a lot. You need to eat things that are essential to live such as things that swim, fly or graze as protein, eat the other fats like nuts, oils, and blubber (I like saying blubber), and things you pick or pull from trees and bushes that are colorful like fruits and vegetables. The rest is up to you to either replace white to brown or toggle back a little or a lot of anything sugary. When you put this at the forefront, add the moves you do every night, taking control of what you eat will eventually lead you to leverage the tools to become healthy and fit.

Tomorrow night, I want to take another trip, but this time we will be going back to the future to give you a glimpse of what would happen if you never came across this journey. On that note, please get a good deep and long sleep to recharge your brain batteries so you can be energized for the beauty that tomorrow will bring. Good night, my friend, and thank you for sharing your life and time with me.

DAY 11
AGE THE WAY YOU WANT TO

Good evening. I'm glad you're still in charge of your mind and body as we begin to approach the two-week check point of your journey. Let's take a trip into the future for a bit of a reminder as to why you are pushing through. But first, take some time to get your four moves done. Talk to you in a few. Don't skip it because I'm watching you! 🏋️

Great, you're back and hopefully you did them with ease and without any difficulties. Now let's take that trip I mentioned earlier. It's a glimpse of a Holiday future if you quit this healthy journey you're on. The minute you're born, your body is biologically developing and growing every minute. By the time you reach your thirties, your body is fully developed and mature. You have reached the apex of your physiological growth and from this point forward, you begin to show signs of wear and tear as the body begins to age. Think of a new car (sorry, car guy) you just bought which has a brand-new engine, shiny paint, a plush interior and that fresh car smell that brings you joy and excitement. For the first five years you drive the car, you don't experience any mechanical problems and the only expenses are washing it and standard maintenance. Due to the wear and tear throughout the years and perhaps some neglect here and there, things start to break down requiring repair or replacement. It's at that point where you want to focus on being proactive to prolong the life of the car by taking actions to preserve it as long as possible.

Much like a car, you can't stop your body from aging, but you can control how you age. By doing the exercises in this book, along with consuming proper nutrition, you have the tools to grow healthier while growing older. It's really that simple.

Next time you're out in a public space, notice how differently we all age. Some of us look old when we're still relatively young. Others who are approaching their later years appear frail, off balance and extremely vulnerable. And then there is another group of people who seem to defy the aging process all together. They are vibrant, active and physically fit (grumble, grumble!).

What is the deciding factor on who ages gracefully and who ages rapidly? The common denominator among those that appear to have found the fountain of youth is that they have discovered the power of building and sustaining muscle through resistance and strength training. Losing mobility or unable to use stabilizing muscles for joints and limbs will accelerate the aging process. You've heard or know of a loved one that fell and broke their hip which always seems to be the point of rapid decent of medical issues and mental despair. And that is the reason why you do the four moves you do every night.

Healthy aging also requires the consumption of protein because it is essential for your organs, immune system and muscle strength. As the body ages, it loses muscle at an accelerate rate. If you are overweight, the excess pounds can lead to joint and back pain. That will eventually hinder your mobility, which is the reason why so many senior citizens feel depress, vulnerable and helpless.

The other challenge is when people who reach middle age freak out and go through an aging crisis and quickly lose a lot of weight by either eating less or eating differently. They join a gym or club and add walking, running, or hours on a treadmill trying to accelerate weight loss. Many of those, especially women, begin to look sickly, gaunt and frail with noticeable protrusions of bone and hollowness. Although thin, unfortunately the skin begins to sag, wrinkle and the bones begin to weaken and stick out noticeably in the arms, legs, and butt with a smidge of muscle. The reason is a combination of many factors, but primarily not eating enough and therefore a lack of protein compounded with the decline of muscle mass.

There is a balancing act between losing the butt and gut at the same time, while increasing and minimizing muscle loss through resistance training and proper nutrition specifically protein. As we age, we require more protein than our younger self from 20g per meal to 25 to 30g per meal because those who are physically inactive begin to lose as much as 8% of muscle each decade after age 30. The good news is that the four moves you do nightly is designed to not only increase metabolism and burn away your butt and gut, but also maintain and build muscle at the same time. The amount is dependent upon the degree of effort, which is why every seven days the routine changes.

It is imperative to eat the right amount of animal or plant protein at the right time every day. So two giant steaks should do the trick. Right? Wrong. The problem is that protein, unlike white or brown foods, cannot be stored because the body can only hold and process up to a maximum amount of 25g to 30g every two to four hours. Don't worry about how much protein to eat right now. Keep it simple and always have protein at each meal—including with your snack.

Tomorrow, I'll talk about essential fats and how the right type of fat won't make you fat. Have a wonderful night and please turn to the ones you love and tell them how much you appreciate them. Being grateful for those you love and telling them how much you care about them is the key to happiness. Everything else is secondary. Good night my friends and hope you have a deep and restful sleep.

DAY 12
EAT FAT TO GET THIN

Can you believe its day 12 already? I bet you're surprised that you made it this far. Well, I'm not! The fact that you started reading this book indicated to me that you wanted to make a healthy change in your life. Changing long-term bad habits into good ones really does take a village of support. Consider me your village! Now let's do the four moves so we can move on and hear more of my nail biting stories. "Y'all Come Back Now Ya Hear!" 🏋️

Today I had to cut back on the first of the four moves from eight to six because I'm a bit sore from an all-day walking excursion. What is crucially important is that even though I didn't complete it, I took the time to do the actions to ensure I consistently do the moves each and every day regardless. Also, listening to your body is extremely important because you need to begin establishing a body and mind connection to communicate, inform, alert and complement each other. The body's sole purpose is to survive, and it will dynamically adjust and change whenever it feels threatened. That is why when those who go on crash diets lose weight quickly, but soon after, gain it right back and often times become even larger. The body thinks the lack of food means that you are starving so it does everything it can to return to its original state. It also will over compensate because it remembers the shock you put it through and will add some insurance by adding some reserve storage. So to become in harmony with your body instead of against it, you eat enough so it doesn't think it is starving, while slowly making incremental and consistent non-threating changes.

This is a perfect segue to the last essential food we touched on during our trip on the deserted island. The dirty "F" word—Fat. For years, fat has been thought of as a negative and condescending word. The word fat is typically used to identify a body type which is used in a negative connotation. I want to change that interpretation by discussing the other fat that is found in food. Healthy fats are key to a balanced food plan and should be a big part of every meal. The idea that fat will make you fat and clog your arteries is simply not true.

The days of low or reduced fat are over and we are now in the era that sugar, overeating and being sedentary are the reasons for the growing obesity rates. In the 80s, food companies began making foods with less fat and replaced it with added sugar. Saturated fat was considered the gateway to a heart attack. However, research indicates that there is no correlation. At least as of today but still, moderation really is the key. In other words, don't eat a bucket of chicken, but instead, eat a drumstick or two even with the crunchy and flavorful skin. Make sure you have your equal amount of brown alternatives, some fats like nuts or avocados in your salad, other vegetables and fruit for the necessary nutrients to keep you balanced and healthy.

There is a simple formula you should apply to all your meals, which is easy to follow and is guaranteed to get you to your goal weight and health.
Here it is:

- Eat 40% protein
- Eat 40% brown foods and vegetables
- Eat 20% quality fats

Here is an example of a sample list of meals throughout the day based on this formula. After waking up in the morning and getting ready for a fabulous day, drink a cup of water. For breakfast, have two or more eggs (protein) with two or three slices of bacon or sausage (fats) with one slice of 100% wheat toast (brown carbs). Don't forget the cup of java to keep the mind alert. Between breakfast and lunch, have one slice of 100% wheat toast (brown carbs) with natural peanut butter (protein and fats) adding half a slice of banana (fruit) making a mini wrap with a cup of water to wash it down. For lunch, have a chicken breast with brown rice (l/g carb), broccoli (vegetable) and some blueberries (fruit) and a cup of plain ice tea to wash it down. Between lunch and dinner, have a handful of mixed nuts (fats) or some regular Greek yogurt (fats and protein) with blackberries and strawberries (fruit). For dinner, have some spaghetti sauce with meatballs (protein) and 100% whole-wheat elbow pasta (brown carb) with a bucket full of peas (vegetable) and an apple (fruit) and some water. For a snack before bed, enjoy either a handful of nuts or plain Greek yogurt or regular cottage cheese with mixed berries.

One last thing, occasionally treat yourself to a cup of ice cream, a cookie, or even a slice of cake. But just remember that how much of it you eat and how often will depend on how much and how fast and up to how long you want that body you envisioned. When it comes to sugary anything, remember what works so well toward the creation of a healthy habit will be equally as effective to form an unhealthy and unfit habit as well.

To sum it up, fat is your friend. As long as you spread the consumption of essential fats throughout your day and balance them with the other food groups, you have the formula for a healthy relationship with food.

Add your muscle-building moves and keep it consistent and repetitive, then you will achieve and sustain good health for the rest of your life. I'll leave you with a quote that may help you understand the nature of what I am trying to convey. "Give a man a fish, and you feed him for a day. Teach a man to fish, and you feed him for a lifetime." I know a bit overly used but was the best I can come up with. Did I just see you roll your eyes? Okay, fair enough. Have a wonderful night and do me a favor. When you wake up in the morning, feel grateful for having the energy and focus to stay on this journey another night. Talk to you tomorrow and sleep deep and well.

Day 13
WATER YOUR HEALTH AND IT WILL GROW

Almost two weeks into your wellness journey and you're still with me. Hang in there! Congratulations. You reached this milestone because of action. Sure, I've laid out a plan, but it wouldn't have mattered to you unless you took action—and you did.

On this journey, each day is extremely important because it's building upon what you did yesterday, and as time goes on, you are becoming healthier in mind, body and soul. This is about being in control of your mind by following along and learning about how to reach your goals with an action plan that is guaranteed to work. It's guaranteed to work because it stems from conditioning the mind and not solely the body because the way you feel, the way you behave, the way you look at things, and the way you want to become is perpetuated by the emotions of wanting to achieve it. To put it simply, if you stop today then you will go back to a unhealthy and unfit life style, but if you continue, you will become successful not only in health but for all aspects of life. So put the book down (I know it's hard) and let's do the moves right now. I'll meet you on the other side. 🏋️

I am back and that was a bit easier today as opposed to yesterday because I had a nice deep sleep last night. Have you noticed that you remembered the moves without needing to stop and think about them? It has now become second nature. Also, time your moves and notice that these short, but critically important movements, you do each night takes less time than a commercial break. The same can be said of the food choices you make. Now that you're conscious of what you're eating, you can choose healthier alternatives in the blink of an eye.

The last, but not least, food category I want to discuss is in liquid form. You see, water is the perfect liquid for your body because it's essential for your body to function optimally. It complements your solid food because water helps digest protein into amino acids, fats into fatty acids and assist the brown carbohydrates to be released into steady streams of energy. When you were stranded on that deserted island, water was essential for your survival. It also accelerates the burning of the butt and gut and improves the digestion process, which in return, reduces bloating thus you feel good throughout the day. It is often overlooked as to how your gut health has a direct correlation to your mood and happiness during the day. One of the best ways to ward off a "snack attack" is to drink water—plain and clear (yikes). You would think sports drinks with all those claims of electrolytes are good for you, but they are packed with sugar, salt, artificial florescent colors and manmade chemicals that you can't even pronounce. If you are dehydrated, drink water, if you have a headache, drink water, if you are constipated, drink water, you want to flush toxins, drink water, if you want younger skin, drink water, if you have horrendous breath (that's me), drink water. H2O is really the fountain of youth!

Now let's chat about other liquids that you may drink that can contribute to the size of your butt and gut. Being a realist and understanding the dynamics of human behavior, you are going to drink other things than just water. As you know, this journey is about awareness so the first thing you need to do is be mindful of the liquids you consume. Start slowly by replacing just one of your sugar-laden drinks with a glass of water. How does that feel? Does it make you full?

Reduce cravings? Allow you to eat less at a meal? Awareness is key to change, so every time you drink water instead of reaching for a different beverage, note how you feel—physically and emotionally.

Time to move on to the "liquor" talk. No, I'm not the party pooper that will kill your happy hour or your backyard barbeque beers, but your goal is awareness for both creating new habits and adjusting old ones. First the bad news. Alcohol immediately stops your body from using your butt and gut for energy, disrupts proper metabolism and inspires fat cells to multiply. The good news is that you don't have to give up alcohol, you just have to befriend moderation. Like anything "bad" for you, overindulgence and a pattern of consistency that harm your body are not your friends. I know, easier said than done but at least you are now aware of what is happening to your body when you drink alcohol, it puts you in the driver seat to begin controlling your choices and intake.

Finally, let's turn to soda and juice. Don't totally blame yourself if you drink a lot of sodas and juices because the beverage industry has had a huge influence on your habit. Data reflects that obesity in children and adults has risen in direct correlation with the rise in sugary beverage consumption. And while juice might seem like an odd culprit to the growing obesity rate in the United States, consider this: a 12 ounce juice box contains about 10 packs of sugar! To put it in perspective, if you only drink one can of soda or juice a day and you replace it with water or a non-sugary drink, you will lose —about 15 to 20 pounds in one year alone!

When I eventually stopped drinking soda, I lost 20 pounds of fat relatively easily from my butt and gut. I feel your emotional challenge through this journey because I am simultaneously working on my food challenges as well. As far as liquids, I am reducing the sugar in my coffee, trying to eliminate diet soda due to its many negative effects claims and removing all the trans-fat additives in my creamer. Remember: To sustain longevity so to be in control of your body for a lifetime requires baby steps to permanently change your behavior. If you want to lose weight faster, then make more dramatic adjustments in your food plan. If you want to take it easy, choose moderation and still enjoy your favorite beverages now and then. I recommend the latter since this is a life time marathon and not a 40 yard dash quick fix.

Tomorrow, be aware of what you drink and eat throughout the day and make one change by replacing a food and/or drink with a healthier choice. Starting is half the battle, so give it a try and if you can make that one change then you are on the road to your habit goal. Goodnight and get ready to celebrate a huge milestone coming up.

DAY 14
CELEBRATE YOUR MILESTONE WITH MINDFULNESS

Its day 14 and you have reached a major milestone so congratulation as this is deservingly a huge accomplishment. You are now one of the 5% in the world that is taking charge of your health, fitness, and most important, your life.

There is a 222 (two, two, two) achievement milestone where the 2's represents two days, two weeks and two months. The first 2 means you have reached the two-day mark and have overcome the challenge of getting started and sticking with it for 48 hours. Most people don't accomplish their dreams because they are unable to simply start the action needed to achieve the goal. If you overcome the first two days then you won half the battle and are now striving toward the second two-week-achievement milestone.

The second 2 means you have reached the two-week mark—which is what you did today. You not only got started, but you made it through the hurdles and challenges of resistance to get closer to your goal. Just reaching day 14 is proof enough that you can do this and are capable to continue on until you progress to your desired outcome.

The third 2 means you have passed the two-month milestone, which solidifies that the routine has become a permanent part of you and the chains of resistance have been wholly removed. You have carved a new habit into your brain and going forward will be as basic as brushing your teeth or getting dressed in the morning.

Each day you are extending and enhancing the newly formed pathway into your subconscious mind, as you continue to repeat the thoughts and actions every day. Today, it's time to kick up your movements to the next level so that your body and mind remain challenged while avoiding a plateau. You will continue to do the four moves eight times, but you will be doing it twice rather than once with a 30-second rest in between. Let me repeat the instructions.

- Do the four moves as you have been doing (no change)
- Eight times for each move (no change)
- Take a 30-second break between sets (no change)
- Do the four moves once again (CHANGE – nightly moves x 2)

Take your time because you want to formulate and maintain proper technic. As each day passes, it will become easier to do as the body and mind will adapt and you will eventually be able to do them all with ease. Let's do the moves right now. So, breath in at the starting position, breath out during the end, do the moves with nice and slow movements with a 30-second rest between the two sets, doing each move eight times. Meet you back here in a few minutes so we can talk further about the benefits of affirmation and accomplishment. 🏋

How did that feel? It was a bit more challenging, I know, but it still only took three to four minutes from start to finish, which is less time than a commercial break. By the way, don't feel discouraged if you have difficulties with a particular move. If you are unable to complete it, that's fine, but it is critical to go through the motions even if you are only able to do them halfway or even doing one of each move. I understand that we are all different and at different stages, but the goal is not to make you suffer but to create a habit of doing them every day without falter. The three minute time you do of exercise each day is an investment in your future. Period. Soon it will become second nature, and you will realize that it was the best thing you ever did for your life. Trust me, it will get easier and you will be grateful!

As I mentioned earlier in this book, your journey is about rewiring your brain (again?). Most weight-loss programs require sacrifice, displeasure, time and suffering, which makes them very difficult to sustain. However, the journey you are on with me is about subtle changes that's consistent, while challenging as you are trying to carve a new lifestyle change into your nightly routine. Your brain is beginning to re-wire itself, shedding unhealthy habits and making imprints of the new healthy ones. Rewiring can occur in the brain at any age—young or old. Learning may come easier to children, but that doesn't mean as we age we can't learn new things. In fact, learning is the gateway to the fountain of youth. Today's neuroscience studies have proven that stroke victims can recover since the brain is pliable enough to create a new pathway and shut down the damaged route. Just to substantiate your efforts, the scientists concluded that nutrition and exercise are equally important during recovery and will help reduce the risk of another stroke.

My father was 85 years old when he had a stroke and lost substantial memory including the name of my son and trouble with mine. However, through practicing the methods I've outlined in this book thus far, he has regained his memory strength and improved his overall health. He's in his 90's (2019) and still sharp, active and mobile.

New imaging technology (fMRI) can visually see real-time brain activity that shows how the brain rewires itself. They are now able to see how the brain changes from moment to moment as the connection between the wires increases in strength by repetitive actions with dependability over time. This applies to your daily moves, as each day you are building upon these new pathways and reinforcing them through repetition. You are also rewiring the eating behavior simply by being aware of what you eat and its effects and making adjustments that complement the moves you do each night. The more days that pass, the more you are strengthening your brain to reroute from old habits to new ones.

As always, it's time for our daily discussion about food. Tonight, let's go out on a virtual dinner to a Chinese Restaurant. Start by choosing dishes with shrimp, fish, pork, beef and/or chicken with unlimited broccoli, snow peas, bell peppers, mushrooms, and carrots. Order tea and enjoy it throughout the meal. Portion control is extremely important so go ahead and order fried rice, but use a small soup bowl as your measuring cup. That will help you stay in control of the amount of food you consume. End the dinner with slices of oranges and crack open and enjoy a fortune cookie. Although the food may not have been the healthiest, you selected dishes and ate portions based on your awareness of consciously making healthier choices. You see, this journey is not about food punishment or deprivation. It's about awareness and making healthy choices that will benefit your body in the long term. You can apply this idea of conscience selective choice to any eating situation you encounter. Whether it's a fast-food restaurant, a wedding, a working lunch, a date night or a party, you are in control of the foods you decide to enjoy.

Before you go to sleep tonight, look in the mirror and tell yourself how much you love and appreciate yourself, your significant other and your family. Be thankful that you are blessed. May you have a deep and rested sleep so we can explore new adventures together tomorrow?

DAY 15
EAT AND PLAY LIKE A CHILD

What day 15 means is that you now have the basic knowledge of what to do, how to do it and why. You learned and mastered proper techniques for each move and are now entering the next level of challenging your body to respond and adapt.

By this point of the journey, you are well aware of why you are on this journey and the purpose of doing an action each and every day. So it is extremely important that you show up consistently from this point forward and do the moves without missing a day to literally reinforce and solidify the new brain pathway you created.

Also, you know how to be in control of your eating behavior, and it is a matter of when you want to decrease your butt and gut and by how much. Each is dependent upon the number of food selections and substitutions you make and if you make the effort to continue doing the moves consistently every day, you will see results.

This way of life mirrors the way martial arts measures progress by doing specific moves over and over until it becomes instinctive and automatic. Each mastery of a set of moves is measured by belts from white, yellow, purple, brown and eventually black when you master all of the technics and mental instilments. The process of becoming a black-belt master is simply doing what is called "KATA," which in Japanese means "form" that entails not only body conditioning, but specifically the conditioning of the mind. In order to advance to the next belt level, you are required to practice, focus and memorize a set of moves and doing the same move repetitively until it becomes second nature without thought and recall. Once you achieve the level of black belt, from that point forward, you use what you learn to develop your own style and continue to practice for conditioning purposes. Even at the highest level, you continue to do the KATA's repeatedly, as it engrains a consistent mind conditioning and spiritual clarity to ensure a lifetime of mastery.

As you go through the process both in martial arts and on this journey, the continual daily practice is applicable to other life goals and is always dependent upon your efforts and ability to invoke the power of progression and consistency. The art of mental conditioning through practice, training and the mastering of technical accomplishment have lasted for thousands of years and continues to be practiced today. That is the core philosophy and foundation of the Japanese people that have enabled them to overcome so many historical devastations yet continue to rebuild, progress and thrive.

I have not yet spoken about the aerobic side (energy-generating process) as opposed to anaerobic (lactate formation) movements on purpose. They both promote weight loss and experts advocate doing both, but for your immediate requirement, the anaerobic movements you do each night will be your primary focus. Aerobic movements such as treadmills and long marathons may not necessarily be good for you as they promote muscles loss and joint stress and can be extremely strenuous and difficult to do. Although you burn calories during the one hour of continuous walking and running, no further metabolic benefit occurs soon after you stop, as opposed to moves you do each night. The nightly moves target both muscle growth and metabolic (calorie burning) conditioning, which the body continues to burn calories during the recovery hours of sleep and the morning thereafter until you repeat the cycle again. I'm getting serious now!

The goal is for you to condition yourself and apply what you discover throughout the journey to achieve maximum effectiveness with the limited time that will last a lifetime. You must consider maximizing time without hindering your ability to continue and sustain the behavior. There are ways to accomplish what took one hour to complete down to only five minutes that can achieve the same calorie-burning results.

Before I get into the nuances of this form of exercise, let's do the 4 moves two times right now so I can get brain clarity to explain this overlooked activity. I'm going to count in Japanese while doing the moves to keep the karate theme going so please follow along and I will meet you back before you can say "sweep the leg and show no mercy." Remember, four moves, eight times and a 30-second rest between the two sets and breathe. Go! 🤸

Do you know that children are the best aerobic trainers in the business? No kidding. Have you ever watched kids at a playground? (not in a creepy way). When observing a child playing at the park, they are constantly exerting short bursts of energy by running really fast and then stopping. Then they climb up as fast as they can, rest for a moment, call someone a butthead, then jump off and run to the next swing or equipment.

What they are doing is called High-Intensity Training or HIIT for short and those kids who play at the playground consistently typically maintain a healthy weight. Additionally, all that pulling, squatting, lunging and pushing to get up and down the playground equipment are simultaneously building muscle each and every school day.

Many researchers suggest that traditional long runs or hours on the treadmill can actually be harmful to your heart, bad for the mind and contribute to muscle loss. So if you are doing this now or thinking that it is the way to go, it would be a good time to pause, not start, or just stop altogether. What occurs during this type of aerobic exercise is that it begins to slowly damage your heart muscles due to overexertion, releases damaging hormones much like when you become overly stressed, and although you may be burning calories, you are also depleting muscle.

So, what we have to do to avoid all these damaging results from long workout sessions is to be a child and do the things exactly as how the kids do at the playground during their short recess time. Short intermittent bursts of running or climbing without stressing any of your joints for up to one minute and resting for two to three minutes. Then repeat that for as many times as you feel comfortable, no more than three cycles.

We can also learn a lot about good nutrition by watching children eat. My son eats one to two eggs, 100% wheat pancakes, milk and berries for breakfast, which helps him focus for school. During his lunch hour, he eats a balanced school-sponsored nutritional meal with morning and afternoon recess snacks, along with his balanced dinner at home. I make sure I put corn in his meals for audit purposes (sick dude!). His morning snack will consist of string cheese with some carrots and water, while his afternoon snack is whole-oats cereal or baked goldfish crackers, apple and yogurt. An occasional sugary treat is sneaked into his lunch box on random days and promises to eat them after he finishes his lunch. Yeah right!

If this sounds familiar, that's because it mirrors the six-meal protein, carb and fat eating routine we discussed earlier. Kids get cranky and sleepy when overly hungry and if they miss the morning and afternoon snack they tend to eagerly want to eat sugary snacks to supplement this void. So to minimize the stress for the teacher and the kids, they make it part of their mandatory daily routine to make sure all the kids eat healthy snacks during these crucial times to ensure order during class time. That is the same eating practice we discussed that adults should follow and apply exactly the same type of regimen for themselves. Never thought that kids can teach us the way to eat and exercise properly, as they demonstrate daily the secret formula to achieve and sustain a healthy and fit lifestyle.

Speaking of kids, when I reflect back to my childhood, my father would constantly say over and over again that sugar is poison and like many children I just ignored him. Who knew that his repetitive rant (hmm, sounds familiar) was the key to avoid so many diseases such as obesity, type 2 diabetes, metabolic syndrome, and fatty liver, to name a few. It is very disheartening to see my son's classmates munching on pop tarts for breakfast while drinking fruit juices because the parents think real strawberries are included as the label alludes. The approach I took with my son is not to say don't ever eat it, but to tell him what happens if you eat too much of it or eat or drink it exclusively. Sugar inherently tastes good and from the time kids begin eating solid foods and get a taste of it, they will constantly ask for it whenever they can. This applies to adults and demonizing it such as my dad did and saying never eat it is not an effective way of managing the consumption of sugar. Throughout our journey so far I've never stated not to eat it altogether because like children, we crave it and it tastes good. Unlike children, as long as you know the effects it does to your organs, blood, and body, that knowledge will allow you to be in control of how much and when.

On that note, please continue to practice the focus and awareness of what you eat and continue on with at least one or two substitutions be it food or drink while breaking up the repetition and quantity of sugary anything. Remember, it takes a small change each day that compounds to weeks, years and decades to keep it up so you can and will prevail. Again, have a wonderful night and hopefully, you substituted your brainwashing television news of violence and dismay with quality time with your loved ones. See you tomorrow and have a good night.

DAY 16
TRICK OR TREAT METABOLISM AND INSULIN

Before we go through our eye-opening trip today, let's do our moves so we can be in the right mindset and state of mind as we have purpose and destination throughout the journey. Here comes the broken record so bear with me when I say let's do two sets of the four moves with precision, smooth motions, proper breathing and notice any type of pain or trouble doing them. Can't wait to discuss this with you since it is extremely important to have insight as to what's happening to your body. See you back here in three minutes tops. 🏋️

How did you do? Isn't it amazing that those two sets of moves can cause your body to react by generating body heat and the need to breathe a bit harder? That slight resistance and discomfort are your body burning calories, helping you to move food throughout your body, tear and rebuild muscle fibers, and setting you up as a 24-hour, butt-and-gut burning machine.

Just for fun, let's make a movie together. We already have the cast of characters within our body. There are three main characters and a few supporting actors. The two locations where we set up the camera and shoot the movie is a bustling town called "The Lazy Liver" and the setting is at an active volcano mountain called "Mount Pancreas." All movies need a villain and a hero so we have one dressed in white (as opposed to black) called "Ravishing Refined Sugar" and we have an unsung hero named "Captain Insulin." The land of the Lazy Liver welcomes everybody as long as they have the means and ability to carry several brown packages of precious fuel called Energy. The packages must be delivered to all the villages across the land who need it to survive. These important delivery workers are asked to stick around in a waiting room and are sent off one by one to manage the traffic on the roads so the packages arrive orderly and accordingly. The problem is that there is a band of evil villains led by Ravishing Refined Sugar that disguise themselves as good-hearted transporters that actually cause nothing but havoc to the surrounding villages.

Luckily, there is Captain Insulin, who gets his power from the mighty mountains of Pancreas that combat the villains by using a weapon that shoots bullets made of a special substance called insulin. These villains are good for nothing and their sole purpose is to occupy and crowd the center of these towns and spray graffiti all over the walls with thick yellow goop. If no one stops them, they continue to spray the walls so thick that no one can go through and therefore blocking the energy deliveries from arriving. They choke the town with thick yellow goop and turn it into desolation and despair. The lazy Liver town is the only passageway to get to the other towns and luckily Captain Insulin is watching. He quickly spots the villains and starts to spray them with insulin bullets, which in turn, makes them disappear. But Ravishing Refined Sugar bombards the town with more and more villains, which makes it tougher for Captain Insulin to defend the land. If the cycle continues, eventually Captain Insulin will run out of bullets and this once thriving land begins to whittle away as the villains block the passage way to the surrounding towns. What's left is an unhealthy town with a large collection of yellow goop that slowly degrades the quality of life in the town.

I know, that was a terrible movie, but I hope it simplified the process a bit. Gaining and losing the butt and gut revolves around the quantity and quality of sugar you eat. We are going to use this knowledge and awareness purely and simply to manipulate how you process sugar so to decrease fat cells both outside and inside your body. Your entire body, especially your muscles and brain, needs the energy to think and move by using sugar as fuel. When you eat any type of sugar from fruits, vegetables, brown or white foods, milk, and white sugar, it all gets processed in your intestines and absorbed into your blood. That blood sugar travels to your Liver and like a gas gauge knows how much sugar your body needs and tries to make sure that your sugar tank stays full (glycogen). The body also has reserve tanks for storage and like a car, the muscle is like your glove compartment that stores and uses it for energy when you do things like walking, talking and doing our nightly moves.

When that reserve tanks get filled up with excess sugar and begin to overflow, the body for survival starts storing the excess sugar in the unlimited reserve trunk called the butt, gut and dangerously the organs as well. The quality of sugar does play a role in this metabolic process because the body does not have an automatic shut-off valve and will absorb and store sugar continuously. Also, when the sugar is made up of stripped down refined sugar found in sweets and white foods, it gets absorbed so quickly it spikes up the blood sugar to undesired and unstable levels. Think of it like your car temperature gauge (car analogy again?) where the level should always be somewhere in the middle so not to overheat or be too cold to function properly.

When the blood sugar level is too high, the Pancreas organ will spray a hormone called insulin into the blood to try to bring it down to a safe midlevel. When the level of sugar is too low it causes your body to pull from alternative sources of energy. It will spray a different hormone (glucagon) that enables your body to take from protein, fats, but more important, from your butt and gut. That's when you start to shrink fat cells from both your mid-section and your internal organs thus decreasing the muffin top, beer belly and plaque in your liver, heart, and arteries.

It becomes dangerous when you continually red line the gauge (sorry again) too high with white and sugary foods for a long period of time, causing the Pancreas to burn out and send out low-quality insulin. Soon your body will no longer be able to bring down the blood sugar to a safe level because it gets overwhelmed like Captain Insulin. This causes a condition called insulin resistance and it impacts not only for those who look large but for skinny people who continue to redline the pancreas.

Once you reach this level, your doctor will give you the bad news that you are Type 2 Diabetic. That's why we need to know the difference between the white foods versus the brown sugars and how the liver processes the difference. Also, the moves you do each night help burn the blood sugar from your muscles and refill it by taking it from your butt and gut reserves while you sleep and throughout the following day. The more muscle a body has, the more glucose it can burn to control blood glucose levels.

It has been published by reputable agencies that the daily recommended allowance of sugar is six to nine teaspoons for women and men respectively. It is so easy to exceed the recommended amount because it only takes a small portion of eating high-fructose corn syrup, molasses, cane sugar, corn sweetener, raw sugar, syrup, honey or fruit juice concentrates to exceed the recommended levels. To put it in perspective, if you eat three chocolate cookies at a conference or drink one can of soda for lunch then you are done for the day. If you are like most people, you are probably consuming 20 to 100 grams during the day.

The knowledge in this section will guide you for the rest of your life of how to reach and sustain a healthy mind, body, and soul. Take your time and make small incremental changes and actions and realize that this isn't a short-term goal but a lifetime journey. Enjoy the rest of your night and take control of your life by being aware of what you eat tomorrow and focus on trying to make at least one food substitution. Yeah, I know. I sound like a nagging parent but there is a point to this repetitive annoyance. Be vigilant so not to let Ravishing Refined Sugar villain destroy your village and help Captain Insulin from faltering.

Tomorrow night I'll share an important thing you are doing each day that has been contributing to an unhealthy lifestyle. Don't peek and read on yet. Be eager with anticipation when we meet again tomorrow night. I hope you know I'm kidding! I'll be back. Good Night and sweet dreams.

DAY 17
SLEEP KEEPS THE BODY YOUNG

Good evening and hope you had a productive and focused day. I'm betting that you either thought about or even made one food substitution or sugary food adjustment today. Hopefully yesterday's movie and explanations about how the Liver and Pancreas process white and sugary foods helped explain what is going on in your body. The small incremental changes you make each day are extremely effective because they are mental adjustments that heighten the awareness as to what you eat, what happens when you do, and how much you need to do to improve your health and fitness for tomorrow.

Many people who go on crash diets or go through a boot-camp-style work out want to lose the butt and gut immediately but never address the behavioral habits that got them there in the first place. They are focused and driven because the emotions are high at the beginning and they may lose weight according to the scale, but once the honeymoon is over, the former behavioral habits return. Absence makes the heart grow fonder for foods that are given up during a crash diet. And the boot-camp drill sergeant that screams at you to do 1000 burpees and flip 3000-pound tires are essentially torturing you into submission. Just to give you some evidence that this type of extreme method rarely works, check out the winners of the popular weight-loss reality shows that features contestants losing hundreds of pounds in a matter of months. Most of the contestants regain a large portion of the weight they lost just a year after appearing on the show. Only a few to none are able to maintain such a drastic change in their body fat for an extended period of time.

An unhealthy lifestyle is years in the making. You don't gain 100 pounds overnight. So why should you expect to lose that much weight in a short period of time? But we do. It's our culture of immediate gratification that makes us believe that we can change our habits—and body size—overnight.

As I mentioned at the beginning of this book and then again and again throughout, the goal is not to lose massive amounts of weight quickly for that summer body. The process is to do small incremental changes and make adjustments in what you eat while doing the moves each night so you have a mental and physical transformation. Losing 250 pounds in seven months means nothing if you gain it back in a year. But if you lose a half a pound a month, six pounds a year, and 24 pounds in four years and beyond without instilling pain, sacrifice and improving year after year forever, this is an effective and long-lasting approach.

You are now gaining control of your body and you are beginning the process of reaching what you envisioned because you know what you want, what to do, why you do it, and how much of it you want to do. Unless you have a condition (i.e. thyroid, hormonal imbalance) that prevents you from becoming healthy and fit, learning, discovering, and understanding the cause and effect of food, the importance of movement and the purpose of building muscle are the only ways to be in control of your mind and body.

On that repeated note, it's time again to take control, but let's sing while doing this to make it a bit more interesting. Let's sing a classic theme song that you may remember that appropriately counts off the same amount of repetitions you do for each move. It goes something like "One, two, three, four, five, six, seven, eight, something, something, something, something incorporated." Okay, I butchered that song and not my best work (if any), but if you can recall where that song came from, let me know. Anyway, let's do the moves with or without the song right now so we can make all our dreams come true for me and you. Okay, I need to stop. Seriously, remember to do the four moves eight times each with a 30-second pause in between the two sets, breathing in at the start and breathing out at the end. If you just mumbled, "I know already", then my work is done. So on your mark, get set and go now. See you in a bit. 🏋️

Okay, I struggled through it today because my thighs are a bit sore from squatting while gardening, but pushed through it. I'm also sleep deprived as my son woke up several times last night making things a bit more challenging, but I did it. That is a perfect segue to the next topic of reasons why I struggled to do the moves today.

It's called sleep deprivation, and it can negatively impact the mind and body, including weight gain and muscle loss. Sleep is one additional, and critical, behavior and actionable change you need to institute that will enhance your overall life experiences. It's true that all of us need a minimum of seven to eight hours of sleep, but it is critical for those who suffer from lack of sleep to seek at all cost and change this unhealthy physical and mental state. I understand some medical conditions will require specialized health professionals to resolve but I'm talking about those who electively sleep less than 7 hours including myself.

When you sleep for at least seven hours, your body releases bottled up stress hormones (cortisol) by removing built-up brain poison you accumulated throughout your busy and stressful day. When you don't drain that poison because of lack of sleep, it will fester in your body causing depression, fatigue, headaches, high blood pressure, bone loss, muscle loss and an inability to strive and accomplish. More important, lack of sleep will make your daily experiences less enjoyable and will prevent you from accomplishing great things.

Lack of sleep also has many other negative results beyond health and fitness, such as losing focus during the day and endangering your life by not being vigilant. This will also hinder your food awareness and behavior, diminish your attitude to do the moves each night and cause irritability that may prevent you from improving your quality of life. Lack of sleep makes you hungry for sugary foods, makes you crave white foods like white pasta, potatoes, and rice, and decreases your ability to burn fat cells (metabolism) both during sleep and during the day. Remember through repetition, conditioning and time, you are training your body to change the way you process food based on what you eat, how much you eat and how much you move to accelerate the way you burn calories. Not enough sleep causes negative issues throughout your body and brain functions, waking up the craving hormone to become aggressive at the same time it halts the muscle-building process. So the lack of sleep is basically trumping all you have learned and done so far, thus making it a waste of time unless you train yourself to get at least seven hours of deep REM sleep.

One last critical thing I want to mention is that the purpose of doing the moves repetitively and consistently each night is to create a habit of doing them to increase and save muscle mass to stay mobile for the years to come. If you do not get enough sleep, you will not fully benefit from the changes you are putting into place right now to improve your quality of life. Bodybuilders and fitness professionals know that muscle growth happens not when they lift weights, but soon after during sleep. The growth hormone needed to build muscle releases during adequate repair and recovery sleep of seven-plus hours. So to avoid increasing both visceral organ, butt, and gut fat, as well as combating frail and brittle bones, get at least seven hours of good quality sleep.

You must train your mind and body to consistently sleep and wake up at the same time even on the weekend through incremental adjustments and practice (circadian rhythm). Please try!

If you are struggling with getting the seven hours of sleep like myself, take small incremental steps by making the effort of sleeping five to 10 minutes earlier each day. Slowly and methodically practice this until you reach the magic hours. Since you are not a teenager, there is no need to sleep more than seven to eight hours unless your body is telling you otherwise for those occasional exhausted or sick days. Just a quick note, some people may think that the moves we do may wire you up suggesting you will have difficulties with sleep due to endorphin hormone release. Rest assured as the intensity is not aggressive enough and falls in line with yoga and meditation exercises that actually promote sleep.

Okay, now I am sleepy and it's close to 10:30 p.m. and since I need to wake up at 5:30 a.m., it's a perfect time to hit the hay and get some shut-eye. I'll probably toss and turn for about half an hour, so tomorrow I will start this ritual at 10:25 p.m., 10:20 p.m. and 10:15 p.m. so to begin the process of training my internal clock.

On that note, have a wonderful night, try again tomorrow to make your food adjustments and feel the joy of accomplishment of day 17., And remember that whatever changes you make, be it big or small, they are all positive actions toward a healthy and fit life. Don't be a passenger in life, be the driver. Good night!

DAY 18
A FRUITFUL WAY TO A HEALTHIER LIFE

Good evening, and I hope you began the road toward seven hours of sleep last night. Perhaps I stressed you out by making you think too much about getting enough sleep that you couldn't fall asleep (so sorry!). Before you lie down, let's do the four moves two times so we can add the muscle and fat-burning deposit to the compounding interest you have invested in for the past 17 days (sorry, finance dude). See you back here in less than it takes to brush your teeth. 🏋️

Good, you made it back to the future. It took me four minutes to complete the four moves two times with a 30-second rest in between. To be honest, I didn't feel like doing the moves tonight but I pushed through, and I'm glad I did. That barrier you feel that prevents you from doing or continuing something is only a brief three-second thought. However, that three seconds can end your journey to the quality of life you deserve.

Just remember that the feeling of resistance, for both the moves and food changes, is just temporary. And if you push through then it will change your life in so many wonderful ways. This skill can be applied to everything in life you want to achieve. The body is just a byproduct of your mind, and you control your behavior and habits that lead to achievement and success.

By the way, if you felt any discomfort on your knees when performing the sitting-down-standing-up moves, stick your butt out more on the descent as you sit. Pretend you are an Olympic ski jumper tucking the sky polls under your arms and bending slightly over to make that stand right before your big ramp jump. You can also modify any of the moves by using a chair instead of a bed, going half way up or down if you feel discomfort, go slower if the moves are challenging and taking a longer break if you feel like you're winded.

Everyone starts this journey from a different physical and mental perspective. Even if you're doing this with your twin, there are so many factors between the two such as genetic makeup, hormonal reaction, diet composition and environmental influences of lifestyle. Each of us is different in so many ways including how your body reacts to certain foods, the rate of building muscles, or how your hormones react to eating white foods and sugar is individualized based on your own distinct biology and physiology. There are fundamental similarities based on body science about certain foods, how the body will process them, and how the mechanics of hormones work. Fundamentally, they are present in all of us but the rate and sensitivity are dependent upon the individual makeup and genetics.

One key indicator on a physical level regardless of gender, ethnicity, or where you live is that your body reacts to food and exercise based on your body type. You are either shaped like an apple, banana, pear, or a combination which determines how and where you store the majority of fat cells.

- The banana body is usually tall and very skinny and has a problem gaining weight, so I'm sure they are not on this journey with us.
- The pear-shape body, which is the majority of us, is really an upside-down pear that will flip as we age as we localize body fat cells around the butt and gut. Pear-shape bodies although can hide body fat better until they gain to a point where they

begin to look disproportional causing the muffin top and beer-belly appearance.

- The last shape is the apple, which are body types that are typically short in stature and distribute fat cells evenly throughout the entire body. Since apple bodies are short in height, they tend to look stockier and rounder. When they increase either fat or muscles, it tends to be more pronounced even if it is the exact amount the pear shape gains. Apple shapes are more sensitive to white foods, sugary treats and beverages, including alcohol. It's tough to be an apple but they give the best hugs.

Those who are apple shaped will need to eat fewer carbohydrates than the pear shaped. In fact, up to 25 percent less for each of your three main meals. The ideal portions are 40 to 50 percent protein and the rest with equal shares of brown carbs, vegetables, berries and good fats. Women, especially as well as apple-shaped bodies, are especially sensitive to carbohydrates. The amount of white foods and sugary anything you eat has a direct effect on your ability to decrease the butt and gut. If you minimize a little, it will mean small to no loss. Reduce a lot, it will mean moderate loss. Eliminate all together, it will be a massive reduction.

The same applies to the pear shapes, but the food percentage is roughly 40 percent brown carbohydrate selections, 40 percent protein, and the rest with healthy fats, vegetables, berry fruits, 100% whole-wheat grains and a handful of your favorite nuts in between meals.

These percentages are just guidelines. You need to become a scientist and experiment with different types of foods and percentages, what and when you eat at certain times of the day, determine your sensitivity by increasing or decreasing carbohydrates and even how your body responds by slowly decreasing your sugary foods and liquids. The golden rule is never starve yourself by decreasing your calories below the recommended allowance, as your body will react by slowing down your fat-burning hormone release. The result of eating less than what your body needs will only make you gain weight, weaken your immune system, eat up your muscles, and make you tired, unhealthy, weak and frail. Don't be in a rush and don't weigh yourself every day because expecting quick and immediate results will only cause discouragement. Being older, you know that anything worth anything takes time which involves action, adaptation, some failure, learning, progress and finally success.

So the message here is to start slow, focus, move forward one step at a time, fight and nudge over the mental barriers, be consistent and repetitive, don't beat yourself up, make incremental changes and try to enjoy the journey. Making lifestyle changes will take time. Your body has adapted to the eating and lack of movement, and it will resist you at every step. So it will require subtle and small incremental changes to avoid any drastic sacrifice and mental resistance. This can be accomplished by slowly and progressively adjusting along the way the nightly moves until you find the balance that will stick with you for the rest of your life.

To sum it all up, we are all different. However, we can all benefit from applying the principles laid out in this book. Continue to strive to become aware of what you eat and focus on food replacements of sugary foods, drinks, and alcohol, get at least seven hours of sleep and enjoy each and every moment of your day. See you tomorrow.

DAY 19
CHANGING HABIT ON YOUR TERMS

I can't I believe we are at day 19 already and hope you're enjoying the journey as much as I am writing it. If you joined me from the beginning of the book and have followed along with the nightly moves, you have completed 812 individual moves on this 19th day. Consistency is your best friend, and you are reaping its rewards.

You now understand that there are only a few simple mental thoughts you need to focus on, two simple foods you need to concentrate on, and four moves you need to do each night. Your awareness of food and what it does to your body has enabled you to become the captain of your ship. A ship does not quickly respond like a race car when moving left or right, but each incremental adjustment in one direction will eventually reach that island you only thought of as Fantasy (get it?).

Speaking of moving, it's that time again to do the four moves twice with a 30- to 60-second rest breathing on the way down and out on the way up. This time around, imagine you are holding five-pound weights in each hand as you do each move. Do move one with your invisible dumbbells in each hand while you go through the motion of sitting and going back up (squats). Then again on move two as you lean towards your toes with the pretend weights by your side as you look up at the ceiling (deadlift). Do the same with the third move doing a dumbbell curl while pushing the weights upwards and downwards as you are mimicking a weightlifting exercise (curl and military press). Virtual dumbbells not needed when doing the last bed push up move (bench press).

The purpose of the imaginary dumbbells is to prepare your mind when you get to the final level later on the journey. If your significant other is watching you, then have them join along and ignore their critical comments and see how they respond physically. If they say that it was easy and a waste of time, then answer by saying it is not the intensity of doing the moves, but the repetition of doing them. Their comments just affirm that the moves are easy but what they don't know is that they are progressive and simple by design to trick the mind to follow along without much mental despair and resistance. Perfect strategy to create a habit, so grab your invisible weights and let's do it. See you in a bit. 🏋

Just finished and I have to admit that I am breathing a bit harder, but not enough to affect my ability to go to sleep. Because the moves are progressive and a bit more effort is required, it may disrupt your sleep. If so, do the moves 15 minutes earlier than your usual time and incrementally adjust backward until you find your sweet spot.

Here's a quick tip. If time permits, take a quick hot shower or a nice hot bath before going to sleep. In Japan, taking what's called "Furo" or a steaming hot tub soak before sleep is thought to help the fat-burning rate and also encourage a deep, relaxing sleep.

I had my first "Furo" when I visited Japan in 1977 and have been following the tradition for more than 40 years. It takes a bit of time to get used to the very warm water and feeling the body temperature rise soon after, but once you become accustomed to it, you will sleep deeply throughout the night. Soon after the hot shower or bath, the body will use energy to cool your body down causing you to get a bit tired. Once the cycle comes to an end, hit the hay and you will sleep like a baby.

Back to day 19 and making adjustments to alternative foods and minimizing sugar consumption (again?). Cutting back on sugar is hard, and it might be one of the hardest things you ever do. Sugar addiction is real, so don't blame yourself for the cravings you have constantly. Let me share my own experience with sugar addiction.

I was extremely unhealthy throughout my 20s and 30s, disregarding the long-term effects of bad eating habits. I believed I was invincible with an attitude that I will live forever. Then, middle-age happened and the reality of mortality hit me hard. I became very anxious knowing I had developed such bad eating habits and that they were wreaking havoc on my health. Old sports injuries were coming back to haunt me. I was gaining weight and felt less mobile. My endurance was decreasing, and I found that doing mindless tasks like carrying in the groceries got me winded and tired.

I knew from that day forward that the old ways of caffeine pills, fad diets, butt-master gadgets and gym memberships were not going to help me going forward. I realized that managing my food intake was purely a mind game of strategy and tactic, which had nothing to do with the body. I applied what I learned in Business School toward health and fitness and used the concept of dollar-cost averaging to sustain my new eating plan for the long run. It worked for me and it can work for you, too. The reason why I selectively chose to target the audience for those near or have reached or passed middle age was that you have many years of real-life experiences under your belt. The journey can only work for those who have already figured out that anything worth anything takes time and effort to achieve lasting results.

This journey will take time not only because you will need to make small incremental changes, but you also cannot afford to drastically disrupt or sacrifice your daily life. You now have reached a time in your life of "I have to" as opposed to "I should." You have only two choices. One is to do nothing and accept the need for medication, walkers and loss of mobility or take action as you are today to become healthy and fit from this point on.

All it takes is subtle behavior changes, be it new or old, done every day until you establish a habit that is progressive, easy, quick and long lasting. Chip away and be patient, as it takes time for the body and mind to train your fat-burning ability (metabolism). It took me two years to retrain the body to respond and reverse 20 years of habituation. Being eager to see quick results is human nature, especially today where everything is instant. When it comes to your body, slow and easy at the beginning is the way to go.

Take notice or write down of all the things that are made from refined flour or sugar that you consistently eat. Then, pay special attention to the day and time you eat these foods so you can see a pattern. For example, if you have a routine of stopping by your favorite coffee shop to get coffee and an apple fritter (yum) each morning before going to work, then write that down.

Now that you are armed with this information, you may feel pumped up and determined not to get that apple fritter. When you wake up the next morning regretting that you didn't go to sleep earlier and feeling the morning grump, like a zombie, you unconsciously take the same morning route to the coffee shop and order that same coffee mocha and shoot, the apple fritter again. You begin kicking yourself soon after eating it, telling yourself you will definitely refrain from ordering it tomorrow. What happened to that feeling of taking charge since knowing the effects of eating that donut and that convincing thought of just stopping?

You've conditioned yourself to take the route and order the same donut for years and now its engraved deep in your brain. It is not about the physical need that is wanting the response, but the mental need to satisfy the expected emotions that have successfully given you satisfaction over and over each morning. The joy of eating the donut doesn't happen when you eat and finish the donut, the excitement happens during the anticipation of eating it. The conditioning is similar to how they train animals as they repetitively have them do a specific trick to get a treat. The animal becomes overly excited anticipating the treat and is conditioned to be motivated to consistently do the same trick automatically without thought. I know, you are not a trained seal but you get my point.

The night before when you were determined to not stop at the coffee shop or not order the donut will not work because removing your freedom is like ruining your happiness by taking away your right of anticipating and receiving joy and pleasure. That process is advantageous when the conditioning of the mind offers you a positive outcome like practicing and playing a sport or reading this book every night (wink). Not so positive when eating a donut every day that effects your health. So what to do?

Using force to stop and rely on self-control is like going against the grain within the mind. The brain will do everything it can to go back to what it finds comfortable and familiar so to achieve pleasure and meet expectations. You are no longer in charge as the area of your brain that you trained cannot be accessed or convinced to stop. The target of breaking the bad habit is to make slight changes to the routine, but not in a negative way of giving up something that requires willpower but just tweaking it a little that still fulfills pleasure and satisfaction. That may seem trivial at first, but a habit is something you do every day at the same time and the same way that expectedly gives you fulfillment from your anticipation.

Once you acknowledge this repetitive act, you will need to make a tiny adjustment to make a blip to the pattern. For example, because the majority of the joy and excitement happens during the anticipation of going to the coffee shop and eating the donut, you can just eat half to satisfy the expected pleasure. May take several attempts but all you need is to do it once. You can eat the other half when you get to work or eat it for dessert. You may think that you are still eating the entire donut anyway so what is the difference but you are slowly changing the pattern by disrupting the mind with unexpected and unfamiliar actions. Don't worry about calories right now as we are concentrating on working on tweaking behavior. The mind will become confused and will either try to get back on track or begin to adjust itself to the new routine. Your thinking side of your brain steps in and you begin to be in control by knowing that you made the choice of eating half, meaning lessening the unhealthy effects by 50 percent. Either eating half or all or none is still your choice, but it is not denying your freedom of choice while still giving you the control rather than the subconscious controlling you.

I mentioned that I have several habits that I needed to overcome and one was drinking two cups of coffee with hydrated powdered cream with lots of sugar in the morning. I've been practicing everything we've learned on this journey for more than 15 years, and I do the progressive move routine every day, changed white foods to brown, and minimized sugar to only special occasions. Without effort and sacrifice, I am able to stay healthy and fit for the many years, but kept a few habits around such as my trans-fat laced coffee milkshake.

For the sake of the book, I decided to apply the principles of making incremental changes to my behavior through substitution and routine adjustments. I started off by using a different creamer, but that didn't work because the taste was so drastically different that I resorted back to my usual creamer. Tenacity is key and not giving up is progressive, so I decided to use liquid half and half instead as I've done when the creamer was not available. Although the taste was not the same, it was familiar and was a small incremental change with a minimal impact that was minimally altering the routine causing the brain to become confused. After a few weeks of making the change, I knew I had the opportunity to kill two birds with one stone, as I decreased the amount of sugar as well. Soon after, I forgot to buy half and half for the week and I happened to be late that morning so I poured black coffee and drank it on the way to work. For the first time after 40 years, I actually tasted coffee in its natural state, and it actually tasted really good.

Since then, I've tried drinking coffee with half and half and sugar but now prefer drinking black coffee. Or maybe I'm always late so I had no choice but it did put a blip in my routine. Regardless, it only took that one day to change the pattern but several attempts to do so. That is close to 40 years of a habitual behavior that I couldn't break until I started making small behavioral changes on my terms.

Even the writing of the book was based on the same principles of doing something every day at the same time each morning consistently. I am writing each morning for one hour, doing the moves with you while writing a section at the same time and the same place every day. Seemed like a daunting task at first, but because my purpose for writing the book was driven purely to help others reach a healthy and fit lifestyle, soon it became a habit that I enjoyed doing throughout the process. Hopefully, this makes sense and the method can be applied immediately as it is a trial-and-error process. It will take time by repeatedly trying different alternatives and substitutions until you find what fits your individual taste and lifestyle.

Tomorrow, I want to touch a bit more on what most people innocently do wrong when it comes to aging by explaining how to avoid them for the rest of your life. And I have a surprise announcement that you will appreciate. See you tomorrow night and wish you a day of energy and enjoyment.

DAY 20
CONSISTENCY IS YOUR FRIEND FOR LIFE

Today is a day of celebration because you are successful for taking action to lose unwanted pounds and for your efforts to formulate a consistent routine. You have knowledge about how and what to eat and understand the concept of compounding through repetition. The journey did not focus on the traditional approach of cutting calories or doing strenuous exercises. Instead, it focused on healthy consistency and duplication.

A paradigm change doesn't happen overnight and normally takes time to transition into it because it involves replacing deep emotional behaviors with unfamiliar activities—and trust. There is a reverse engineering phase that takes time to understand its pattern so you can disrupt it and change it. The mind is what got you unhealthy and unfit, not the body. Rather than a short-term sprinter like approach, you've taken on a marathon-like training methodology during this journey. And now you're reaped the benefits—for life.

As you go forward, continue to build a relationship with your mind and body, but most importantly, take action and move forward toward your vision. This is the same principle for anything at which you want to be successful. Small, consistent steps will lead you to triumph for the long term. Speaking of small actions, it's time for us to do the moves you've been mastering for the past three weeks. However, this time keep track of how long it takes you to complete them. It's not a race, but I want you to be fully conscious of how little time and effort it takes to make big strides in your good health. So two sets of four moves doing each move eight times with a 30-second rest in between sets, while breathing in at the start and out at the end of each move. 🏋

While doing the moves using a slow and smooth technique, it took me exactly four minutes to complete. How long did it take you? If it was less, then you will want to slow it down a bit to ensure you have proper rhythm and pace. Although I have degenerated lower back discs from an unresolved injury, I was still able to do the moves without any pain or discomfort. My body temperature rose which means my muscles are being fired up due to the physiological process of building them and burning of the butt and gut. I can't tell you how critical these moves are, and as you progress into the future, it will increase the probability that you will remain mobile for the rest of your life.

When talking with the elderly about aging, many agree that the most difficult part is the loss of balance and mobility. That doesn't have to happen to you, as you now have the knowledge to be proactive instead of reactive. You can increase muscle, stamina, energy, and an overall good feeling by taking charge of your health—today . The road to the straight and narrow is to be repetitive and consistent with everything that adds value to your life, and by using the passing of time to work for you as building blocks for vitality.

Conversely, anything repetitive and consistent you do that adds negative value to your life will cause harmful consequences, making time work against you and creating undesired and often times irreversible outcomes. This applies to finances, relationships, and of course, health and fitness. As you envision your ideal future outcome, learn everything you can about it, focus on small incremental actions toward it, and continue to improve upon it. I know it sounds like a broken record, but this concept is the essence of the book and the secret to many successes so I will continue to remind you of its importance.

You will discover that there is a mind-and-body connection when it comes to health and fitness, where the mind is the primary vehicle and the body does what it is told to do. Instead of thinking "I am overweight" or "I can't seem to lose weight," change your phrasing to "I am in control of my good health" or "I will take action that will help me lose weight." Once you are in control and using what you learned throughout the journey, you can move towards a healthier lifestyle.

This applies to making a habit stick by doing it over and over and over again (like my repeated rants). You've trained yourself to do your nightly moves and be more mindful of what you put in your body each day. At first, your journey may have seemed like an ordinary nutritional guide and an exercise routine. But now you know it's a process of doing an action, focusing on awareness of eating patterns, continuously trying to be conscious of your food choices, and doing it consistently so it becomes a habit.

If you may, I would like to share another corny but true story that may resonate with you or at least, help you fall asleep. Many of you have experienced remodeling parts of a house like a kitchen or a bathroom. I renovated my bathroom with all the bells and whistles you can imagine, including the installation of an invisible glass shower door. The installer recommended I use a glass-cleaning squeegee after every shower to avoid permanent water and mineral deposits. Every time I took a shower I would grumble about what a bad idea it was to get a floor to ceiling glass shower wall and door, as I cleaned it off with the squeegee. What a pain! But overtime I noticed I was getting faster and more efficient at doing it. One day my wife told me there was no need to clean it after my shower because she was going to jump in next. (Get your mind out of the gutter). Without even realizing it, I squeegeed the glass before I got out. It was so automatic to me that I didn't even notice I did it anyway. I knew at that moment that I either never listen to my wife or the act of squeegeeing had become hard-wired into my subconscious. It has happened several times since, so yes, I do listen to my wife (selectively), and yes, doing something repetitive even when it is not enjoyable can and will become a habit.

Another and last example (yeah! Or Boo!) is the challenge of writing and publishing this book. I am not a professional so it seemed like an impossible venture but by following that exact same principles I've laid out for you, I have reached my goal and it is one of the most rewarding things I have ever done other than achieving a healthy and fit lifestyle. Oh, and getting married and having children.

I first visualized writing and finishing this book with the hope of having many of you follow along the entire journey with me. From there, I felt the emotions of helping to change the course of someone's quality of life--forever. That motivated me to write down the first words of this book and start my own journey. To sustain the motivation and move forward, I created a routine that was repetitive and consistent by dedicating one hour a day at the same slotted time every day and never missing a day.

It was difficult at first because I was creating a new ritual that the mind was not used to, and it felt unnatural. Oftentimes, I got discouraged but I continued. There were many points where I faced emotional barriers, but I pushed through them knowing the feelings would only last a brief moment. Sometimes I could only dedicate a few minutes to writing, but I knew I had to keep the consistency going. As time passed, writing became part of my daily life and the effort became second nature, thus a new habit formed. It came to the point where I began looking forward to writing each day, and if I couldn't do it for as long as I wanted, it felt like something was missing. It took 3 years but what mattered is that I accomplished a lifetime goal and learned so much during the journey about the industry and more importantly, getting to know myself and who I am.

I know the message I am trying to spread is so critically important. When you take action and do it every single day, even though it seems impossible, you can—and will—be successful.

The 21-day journey may end tomorrow, but this is just the beginning, not the end. I invite you to continue your journey with me on my free website. It's designed to get you to the finish line—and beyond. Consider it your 24/7 fitness coach that you can tap into anytime, anywhere and for any reason.

The website features:

- Daily fitness reminders to help you navigate through life's challenges with ease
- Food tips and recipes to support your healthy choices
- Breathing and movement exercises you can add to your regime at your own pace
- Mindful activities to keep your brain as fit as your body
- Inspirational stories to support your motivation and dedication to lifelong fitness
- And much, much more

I wrote this book to help people take action and breakthrough their decades-old limitations they set for themselves without even knowing it. My goal for you is to be one of the 50 percent of the population that is not deemed obese and diagnosed with an overweight-related disease.

You are reaching the end of your 21-day journey, but remember, I will always be here to help you get to your end goals. You are the director and the main character of this movie called life, so don't be an extra, be a star. I am so proud of all that you have accomplished! You now have the map that will safely navigate you on any journey you decide to take. Good night, my friend, and sweet dreams.

DAY 21
"THIS IS YOUR LIFE!"

Today is bittersweet, as we've reached the end of our 21-day journey together. You now have the tools to help you on the next part of your journey so you can achieve – and go beyond – your health and fitness goals. In a sense, you're just getting started! Every incremental food substitution you make, every move you do at night, and every choice you make to do something healthy has a compounding effect that's leading you to be in control of your life. It is purely your choice to make it happen and how much you want to change the current state as you are the only one who knows what to do, why you do it and when you want to get there. You are the star and director of this movie called "This is your life," and you are the creator and performer. You're no longer a spectator. You're a lifelong participant. You must first envision your award-winning movie, learn the business as to how to direct and perform, continually learn the craft, execute what you learned, practice daily to condition yourself to face and overcome the challenges along the way, and enjoy the process until you win "Best Picture".

Let's wrap up this book by doing our final moves—twice. I'll meet you back here in a few minutes. See you in a bit, as I am going to follow my advice and do exactly what I just explained. 🙌

As promised, I would like to tell my story if you allow me so to share how I lived the first half of my life and how I used all the adventures we faced during our journey to stay healthy and fit. Fifteen years ago throughout my early to late thirties, I had the spare tire, the sagging man breasts, hump on the back of my neck, puffy face, double chin, legs that rub, and a wide butt and protruding gut. The results of neglect were high cholesterol, high blood pressure, high glucose level, low energy, always bloated, depressed, and the added annual doctor's reminder to watch my diet. I would buckle up and immediately go on a diet, order a salad, order a wheat lawn grass drink, and run on a hamster wheel for hours. Once the fear of death faded away after a week or two, I would ease my way back to my old ways. Sound familiar? I would continue until a calendar reminder pops up prompting me to make the annual physical as the cycle repeats.

The problem was I knew I had to do this but how can I get there. I failed in the past and always went back to my unhealthy ways so now what. Since nothing worked in the past, I needed to approach this differently, so I decided to study the effects of aging and focus on the direct route of aging gracefully. I needed the real deal and avoided wasting any more time, so I began to study until exhaustion everything and anything about nutrition and exercise. This time around being of age, instead of trying to lose weight quickly, I took the approach of creating a routine that I can sustain for the long run. It wasn't about how much I can bench or how much calories I need to cut but how as an older and mature adult achieve it intelligently. I needed to figure out a way to leverage my strengths and come to terms with my behavior limitations. So the one advantage over my younger self-was that I knew that anything worth anything takes time and persistence.

What also resonated being of middle age was that achievement was not about will-power or how much sacrifice and pain I can endure but how I can condition and sometimes trick the mind to repeat an action continuously. It also struck me that to react effectively without much thought and effort requires repetitive practice and steady consistency. I drew from the military, sports athletes, police, firefighters, martial artists, entertainers, and practically anyone who is skilled in their craft.

Each followed a protocol of practicing a technical move over and over until the results are consistent, constant, and automatic. So I took that mindset and just carved out fifteen minutes of allocated time each day and made it a point to block that time from my calendar and use it for health-related exercise and research regardless of work or social demands. I would isolate myself from others and do this routine at the same time every day trying not to miss a day for at least the next two weeks. After several weeks, it started to become my daily routine without much forethought. Each day after became easier and without much mental resistance. It continued for two more months as I then realized that it has manifested into a way of life.

What confused me was that even though I was consistent and put in the work, I didn't notice any change as I weighed myself each day to see the results. Although this was discouraging at first, I knew that reserving this time each day and committing to it was creating a routine which became a void when I was unable to do. So rather than disrupting that newly developed conditioning, I decided to focus the remaining ten minutes on research time alongside the moves to begin searching out why I was not showing any significant results. During my research about building muscles before and after forty, I began to notice a common saying that muscle growth doesn't happen at the gym but in the kitchen. The phrase meant that the formula to become healthy and fit was twenty percent resistance training and eighty percent nutrition accompanied with rest and recovery.

Essentially as explained throughout the journey, one needs a steady stream of protein for building muscles, fats to help curb your appetite and help burn fat, and a focus on carbohydrates selection and management to lose body fat. I eat forty percent protein, twenty percent fats, and the remaining forty percent with quality carbohydrates of fruits, vegetables, and the preverbal brown alternatives. I then began to build a relationship with my mind and body becoming more in tune with how it reacted to certain foods, being more aware of my eating behavior, seeing the effects of the moves that targeted muscle growth and metabolism, and saw the body fat decrease steadily and incrementally. The butt and gut began to reshape from a large pear to a medium pear to a small pear eventually transforming into a healthy and fit body with test results to match. I continued on the same journey which mirrored our journey together from two months to two years working on incrementally making the carbohydrate food substitutions, finding other ways to fulfill any sugary habits, creating recipes that are delicious using brown foods, and continually doing research on the science of the mind and body. I recorded the progress, and the graph showed gradual changes for the first two years but soon after, the body shifted into overdrive, and the graph line showed significant improvement and change. Eight years later while still keeping the same fundamentals and core principles used on our journey, I managed to improve wholly and continually reshaped the body as I got stronger by building more muscle. I have the energy of a teenager, sleep like a bear, and I am always eating. This has been one of the smartest things I have ever done in my entire life, and I kick myself for not being smart enough to start when in my twenties and thirties.

Today, due to excellent test results, I have increased my life insurance to one million dollars, I have more energy than a twenty-year-old, I help psychologist and neuroscientists stay physically fit, and I have executives asking to train them. I have yet to miss the daily moves, and I continue to find ways to make healthier food substitutions even after 15 years. I have applied the same principles we used on other facets of my life. This process as simple as it is has reshaped my marriage of thirty plus years with my beautiful wife by practicing daily the habit of listening, compassion, and respect. I achieved financial success with simple repetitive rituals of paying myself first, applying proven money management techniques, and leveraging the law of compounding interest. The quality of my life has improved one hundred times over and look forward to finding new ways to improve my health, finances, and relationship for the years to come.

Unfortunately, we are at the end of our journey today, but I will forever feel uneasy that maybe it wasn't quite enough and you still need a bit more help. I don't want our journey to end as I have enjoyed every day connecting with you hence why it is not easy for me to say goodbye. I know I have to let you go but remember I am committed to continuing until you and I reach our journey goal of becoming healthy and fit forever. On that note, as I alluded earlier, I created a free website so you can continue on the passage by following the instructions described in the conclusion section below. So before we end tonight, if you need or want to continue with me, please read below, and I will meet you there as we can move on and strive to keep improving upon our lives forever.

CONCLUSION
Join the FREE web site to continue on for 21 more days

I want to take this moment to thank you from the bottom of my heart for sticking with the journey and believing in me. I am also grateful for sharing your heart for our children who need financial and medical help. Your kind gesture will give the underprivileged a chance for a normal and happy childhood. I also want to express my respect for going on this journey and finding the strength to make the change knowing how hard it is to make even one behavior adjustment. It takes a lot of mind battling, energy, perseverance, and commitment to overcome something that crept upon you. So I am inspired by you and others who have faced so many life's challenges yet had the strength to seek out the book and commit to reaching a healthy and fit life. Never give up, pursue your dreams, move forward, and take incremental steps that lead you toward your dream goals. Continue to strive forward and keep creating new ways to build habits for anything that gives you positive results.

I'm going to wrap this book up, but because this is about helping you, I don't feel right leaving you after day 21. I created a website that continues for an additional 21 days with more details and added enhancement to capitalize on what we have learned so far. There is no cost or fee for membership. Once you create your profile, you get exclusive access to fat burning recipes, a comprehensive white to brown food lists, informative training videos, and of course, the additional 21-day journey. If you prefer, you can create an email account using an alias so I can still reach out to you without disrupting you in any way. The email address will never be sold, used for marketing, or shared with anyone and you have the ability to remove yourself permanently from the site at any time. It is important though that you email me at HFF@passionhabit.com to let me know which charity to send the proceeds. On the site, you will find a link on the home page called Children Charities that lists and describes the organization's mission. Click your selection as described on the page and I will forward the proceeds to them.

But before you can enter the site, you will need a password to create a profile which is **7779311**. It is buried here intentionally to ensure you obtain the foundation to be prepared to continue. I sincerely thank you for your contribution, and hopefully we can sell enough books to make an impact on those who need our help. I am also available to help along the way once you finish the book either by emailing me directly or leverage the website. So go now, and I will meet you at *http://HFF.passionhabit.com* and once again strive to improve and become Healthy and Fit Forever.

www.ingramcontent.com/pod-product-compliance
Lightning Source LLC
Chambersburg PA
CBHW021621270326
41931CB00008B/813